I Pick Up Hitchhikers

Edwin T. Dahlberg

I Pick Up Hitchhikers

"I searched out the cause of him whom I did not know"
(Job 29:16)

Judson Press ® Valley Forge

I PICK UP HITCHHIKERS

Library of Congress Cataloging in Publication Data

Dahlberg, Edwin Theodore, 1892-
   I pick up hitchhikers.

   Includes bibliographical references.
   1. Dahlberg, Edwin Theodore, 1892- 2. Baptists—Clergy—Biography. 3. Clergy—United States—Biography. 4. Hitchhiking—United States. I. Title.
BX6495.D25A34   286'.131   [B]   77-25498
ISBN 0-8170-0774-1

To My Wife
VIOLA LOUISE DAHLBERG
"Voila, Viola!"

"I am a part of all that I have met;
Yet all experience is an arch wherethro'.
Gleams that untravell'd world whose margin fades
For ever and for ever when I move." [1]

—*Tennyson*

[1] Alfred Tennyson, "Ulysses," *The Complete Poetical Works of Tennyson,* ed. William J. Rolfe (Boston: Houghton Mifflin Company, 1898), p. 88.

Preface

There is a sentence in the Old Testament book of Job that has always challenged me. Seeking to justify himself in the sight of God, Job cried out in the midst of his excruciating pain and anguish, "I searched out the cause of him whom I did not know" (Job 29:16).

Nothing is more needed in the contemporary scene than that we should acquaint ourselves with the causes of people we do not know. We tend to associate ourselves only with the causes of people we do know, our immediate circle of friends and working associates. Consequently we live in too small a world.

My greatest and most famous teacher was Walter Rauschenbusch, professor of church history at Rochester Theological Seminary until his death in 1918. He said to us students in his class one day that people who travel abroad often return home without having broadened their horizons nearly as much as they might have. This is due in large measure to the fact that even in foreign countries they mingle with much the same social and economic groups they meet with daily back home: businessmen with businessmen, labor leaders with the officials of labor unions overseas, club women with club women, educators with educators, church men and women with representatives of their various denominations or ecumenical organizations in other lands. Persons may return from abroad with a smattering of foreign culture. But basically they come home unchanged, without much change in their opinions, their ideologies, or their ways of life. There may be exceptions. Some people go overboard for the new and the untried in other parts of the world, to the degree that they come back practically denationalized. But others, even though they haven't been changed by their experience, come home to live forever after as citizens of what they consider a new and more exciting world.

One of the better aspects of our generation is that without

realizing it we are following Job's example. We are searching out the causes of people whom we do not know. The male members of our society, for example, are becoming increasingly aware of the injustices done to women, especially in the economic world. One result of the ecumenical movement, likewise, is the developing desire to become more informed about the history and doctrines not only of the particular communions to which we may belong, but also to learn more about the teachings of other churches, whether Protestant, Roman Catholic, or Eastern Orthodox. Evangelicals and social actionists are also entering into dialogue with one another, giving promise of the day when we shall proclaim the whole gospel rather than a partial, fragmented faith.

Much remains to be done, however. We have a long way to go. How ignorant we are of the causes so vital to minority groups, such as the Indians and the blacks. Calling desperately for our attention, too, are the needs of the migrant workers, the aging, the conscientious objectors to war, and the millions of crippled people who have no way of getting into a bus or up the stairways of their churches and other public buildings. If we will but listen, there are coming to us from every direction calls similar to the Macedonian call that came to the apostle Paul when a vision appeared to him in the night: "a man of Macedonia was standing beseeching him and saying, 'Come over to Macedonia and help us'" (Acts 16:9). How we need to respond with compassion to the plight of the poor, the hopeless inmates of our mental and penal institutions, and the victims of hunger and starvation around the world!

Inspired by something of this growing spirit of concern, I decided some years ago to follow Job's example by searching out the cause of the hitchhikers on our American highways. This is only a small segment of our population. Also, it is largely unknown, even though we see outstretched thumbs as we go speeding by in our cars.

Too often we dismiss hitchhikers from our minds as a lot of "hippies and bums," trash that ought to be kept off the roads. Some of them may not be too desirable. But they are human beings just the same—people for whom Christ died. I have found among them some of the most interesting and intelligent people I have ever known: some young, some old; some students, some runaways from home; many out of work, some despairing, and others looking hopefully for better opportunities beyond the horizon, as did the American homesteaders, gold seekers, and frontiersmen before them.

They are worth knowing. So—meet the twentieth-century hitchhikers! I would like to present a few of them to you.

Contents

1

America's Jericho Road

The older people of my generation—I am now eighty-five—react with horror and consternation when I tell them I pick up hitchhikers on the interstate highways.

"Isn't that pretty risky? Even dangerous?" they ask.

These are valid questions. There are some risks. A couple of years ago, a businessman in the Pacific Northwest picked up two girls within the city limits of his community. This is something I would never do. The possibilities of blackmail and scandal are too great. The consequences in this case, however, were of quite another kind. When they were only two miles out of town, one of the girls pulled a gun on him, told him to hand over his car keys, and get out of the car. He was left helpless by the side of the road as they drove away.

We live in a crime-ridden culture. Therefore, I would not advise people in general to pick up hitchhikers. However, it is not on the highways alone that we encounter danger. We can run into a bank robbery when we go into a neighborhood bank to cash a check. Holdups at the supermarkets of our great cities, too, are almost daily occurrences.Therefore,while we must be careful, let us not run scared.

Oddly enough, after eight summers of transcontinental travel alone, driving for many thousands of miles from coast to coast and picking up hitchhikers by the score on every trip, I have not had one unpleasant experience. All my passengers—hippies, students, job hunters, runaway husbands, aging drifters, or local boys just thumbing their ways to the next town to call on their girl friends— have been uniformly courteous and grateful for the lift.

Someone may ask, "How did you happen to start this practice?"

The truth is that as an ordained minister of the Christian church I was having some trouble preaching about Jesus' parable of the good Samaritan. If you will read the story as recorded in the New Testament—Luke 10:25-37—you will readily understand my difficulty. A lawyer in Jesus' outdoor audience asked him what one had to do to inherit eternal life. Jesus came back at him with another question: "What do the Scriptures say about it?" "You shall love the Lord your God with all your heart, and with all your soul, and with all your strength, and with all your mind; and your neighbor as yourself," was the lawyer's reply. "Correct!" said Jesus. "Do this, and you will live."

In answer to the lawyer's further question, "And who is my neighbor?" Jesus then told the story about a man who had been beaten by bandits on the Jericho road, stripped of his raiment, and left half dead by the roadside. Two of the religious leaders of the day happened to come along a little later, one of them a priest and the other a Levite (a priestly helper in the service of the temple). They were religious professionals like some of us. Both of them passed by the wounded man. It was not until a rather despised foreigner came along on his donkey that the injured man got any attention. It was this stranger, immortalized now for nearly two thousand years as the Good Samaritan, who immediately came to the aid of the bandits' victim. He lifted up the man, set him on the donkey's back, took him to an inn after some preliminary first aid, and advanced the innkeeper enough money to pay for the stranger's room and board until he himself would be coming back on his return journey.

Jesus then addressed the crucial question to the lawyer, "Which of the three do you think was really a neighbor to the unlucky traveler who fell among the thieves?" The answer was so obvious that the lawyer could only reply, "He that showed mercy on him." "Go, and do likewise," said Jesus.

I have never subscribed to the theory that the priest and the Levite passed by on the other side of the road simply because they were in a hurry to get to a committee meeting or some other important appointment.

The truth is, they were probably scared. William Barclay tells us in his fine commentary on the Gospel According to Luke that the road from Jerusalem to Jericho was a happy hunting ground for brigands—so much so that in the fifth century Jerome still spoke of it as "The Red, or Bloody Way."[1] Like the highwaymen of our own time, the bandits of the first century were in the habit of using decoys. One of their number would act the part of the wounded man. When some unsuspecting traveler stopped to help him, the others would then rush upon him and overpower him. Knowing this, many a

[1] William Barclay, *The Gospel of Luke* (Edinburgh, Scotland: The Saint Andrew Press, 1956), p. 141.

person adopted the policy of "safety first" when on the Jericho Road. And it made some sense then as it still does today.

Somewhat uneasy myself about the risks involved, I had had the habit of ignoring the hitchhikers I came to along the great highways of America. After my wife died in 1968, however, by which time all three of our children were grown and married, I figured that as a fairly ancient senior citizen it wouldn't make too much difference to the world if I did get "bumped off." Moreover, when one of our sons went overseas as a soldier of his country in World War II, and our other son and his wife went up into the jungles of northern Burma as medical missionaries to the mountain tribes of the Eastern Shan States, within fifty miles of the Chinese border, they all took some big chances, too, as many of the young people of our generation have done in one way or another. Policemen, firemen, doctors, construction workers, do they not all do the same? Why, then, I thought to myself, should I be exempt?

So it was that one beautiful afternoon in northern Wyoming along a lonely stretch of road on Interstate Highway 25 I picked up my first hitchhiker, with some trepidation, I must confess.

He proved to be a weary-looking man of middle age, backpacking his way northward toward the Montana border. As we introduced ourselves, he said apologetically, "I'm just a saddle bum looking for a job on one of these ranches."

"Where from?" I asked.

"From Mississippi," he replied.

"If you are from Mississippi, I wouldn't be surprised if you turned out to be either a Methodist or a Southern Baptist," I suggested.

"Right!" he said. "Though I'm sorry to say I ain't been workin' very hard at it." I had already come to this conclusion, as the odor of alcohol indicated that he had been drinking a bit more than he should. He was in good command of himself, however.

Little by little he opened his heart to me, apparently glad to share his life story. I might say at this point that I never tell a hitchhiker I am a minister unless he asks me what my work has been. It then becomes very natural to have a conversation about spiritual matters. Deep in the heart of the average person—particularly lonely persons as so many hitchhikers are—there is a longing for the Eternal. And in a situation such as I have just described, it becomes easy for the person at the wheel to witness for Christ or to offer some pastoral counsel, since it is the hitchhiker himself who has initiated the situation by asking for a ride.

14 ■ *I Pick Up Hitchhikers*

About fifty miles nearer to the Montana border, my saddle bum friend suddenly exclaimed, "That ranch over there looks like about as likely a place as any. I think I'll try my luck there."

"Fine," I said. "But how about having a prayer together before you go on your way? We probably will never see each other again. I've enjoyed meeting you so much and would like to ask God to bless you in the days ahead."

"OK," was his hesitant reply. "God knows I need it."

So I offered a simple prayer, thanking God for bringing us together and asking him to help this newfound friend in his search for work and above all in living his Christian life throughout all the years to come.

As he shouldered his heavy backpack again, I took the liberty of adding a final word. "Stay close to the Lord now," I said. "Get out your Bible again, and remember what you learned in that Southern Baptist church down in Mississippi."

"Thanks a lot, Reverend," was his reply. "With God's help, I'll certainly try."

My heart ached for him as I saw him go. He had told me during our conversation that his mother had died when he was only four years old. "I hated my father," he confessed. "So when the war came along, I ran away and joined the army. My father died while I was overseas, and I never heard about his death until two years later. I'm sorry about that. Now that I am older, I realize that I was probably not too good a son. He must have had a hard time trying to be both father and mother to me when I was growing up."

I still pray for him. Saddle bums are not necessarily bums. Many of them are wounded men by the side of the road—wounded not in body, but wounded in spirit from their earliest days.

That's how it was—my first encounter with a hitchhiker. Thus encouraged, I have continued over the years to give the men along America's Jericho Road a lift—a lift in the car and, I trust, a lift also in the Christian faith. I have in a sense considered myself a self-appointed chaplain to the hitchhikers on the interstate highways. I consider this a special mission in my retirement years.

It has been a rich and rewarding experience. I have learned more than I can say about this wandering, restless generation. I hope to introduce to you in the further chapters of this book some of the interesting people I have come to know and their attitudes towards life. I look upon America's Jericho Road as one of the most promising yet one of the most neglected mission fields to be found anywhere.

Such a mission is a kind of Johnny Appleseed ministry, dropping a seed of prayer in one likely spot, a verse of Scripture further on, or maybe some pastoral counsel and a bit of hope and encouragement somewhere else. Whether the seed will find lodgment in the mind and soul of a stranger and blossom into flower and fruit somewhere in the wilderness, only God may ever know. But it is a fascinating possibility.

The first hitchhiker on record, so far as we know, was Philip the Evangelist, whose story we can read in the New Testament (Acts 8:26-40).

He was traveling south on the desert road going from Jerusalem down to Gaza, on the way to Egypt. There he met a man of great distinction, known to us as the Ethiopian eunuch, who was secretary of the treasury under Candace, queen of the Ethiopians. He was riding in his chariot on his way home after having been in Jerusalem to worship. He was evidently a proselyte, as a convert to the Jewish faith was known.

Philip was walking along the road as the chariot came along. Suddenly he had an inspiration. We are told that "the Spirit said to Philip, 'Go up and join this chariot.'" Philip ran to the chariot and found the Ethiopian reading aloud from the prophet Isaiah as the charioteer drove him along. Philip said to him, "Do you understand what you are reading?" "How can I, unless someone guides me?" was the reply.

Invited to come up into the chariot and sit with him, Philip began to explain to the Ethiopian the Old Testament prophecy concerning the coming of the Messiah. The upshot of the conversation was the eager decision of the eunuch to accept Christ as the Son of God. "See, here is water," cried the eunuch, as he commanded the charioteer to pull up by the roadside. "What is to prevent my being baptized?" Philip baptized him. They never saw each other again. But the eunuch went on his way rejoicing, as Philip journeyed on to Caesarea.

Thus we have a biblical basis for a hitchhiking ministry. The difference is that Philip, the hitchhiker, was in this case the witness for Christ, and the man in the chariot was the convert—possibly the first convert to Christianity in all Africa. No wonder he went on his way rejoicing!

It has never been easy for me to speak to a stranger or a chance acquaintance concerning his or her relationship to Christ. But we have come to a time when we need to ponder the words of Theodore P. Ferris:

There are just two ways to spread anything in which you are greatly interested. The first is to live it yourself, and the other is to talk about it. . . . There is a strange kind of reticence that has settled upon the Christian movement like a fog bank, and it does not seem likely that the movement will ever really move until that fog lifts. Have you ever talked to one of your contemporaries about the Christian religion? . . . We say that we respect the liberty and the rights of people to think for themselves, and so we do. But there is something strange about reticence when it goes that far and when it comes into the realm of things that presumably we care so much about. We have already seen what Philip found and what he did—he opened his mouth. . . . He preached unto him Jesus.[2]

Once we begin to give our testimony simply and humbly, we find it increasingly easier as we go on. When we are overcome by a sense of our inadequacy in witnessing for Christ, we should be encouraged by the promise he gave to his twelve closest disciples. Reminding them that they would some day be called upon to stand before governors and before kings in their testimony concerning the faith, he said, "Do not be anxious how you are to speak or what you are to say; for what you are to say will be given to you in that hour; for it is not you who speak, but the Spirit of your Father speaking through you" (Matthew 10:19-20).

This promise is as valid when we are speaking to a friend or a neighbor about our faith as it was when the early Christians were defending themselves in court. Let there be an end to our reticence, therefore; let us always remember to pray that the Spirit of the heavenly Father may be speaking through us.

This is my prayer as I try to give my witness on America's Jericho Road—or anywhere else.

[2] Theodore P. Ferris, in *The Interpreter's Bible,* ed. George A. Buttrick, 12 vols. (Nashville: Abingdon Press, 1954), vol. 9. pp. 114-116.

2

A Postgraduate Seminar on Highway 90

The very next day after the experience in Wyoming, I hit Interstate 90 at Billings, Montana. Only a mile or two west of Billings, in a driving rain, I stopped for a young couple heading for Seattle. It was early in May and very cold. It was evident that the young man and his girl friend standing by the side of the road were drenched to the skin. Heeding their desperate thumb appeal, I opened the car door and let them in. They dumped their soaking wet backpacks into the backseat and gratefully crowded into the front seat beside me, directly in front of the heater. I turned the heater on full blast.

"Thank you for stopping," said the young man. "What a rain! It sure feels good to get into a warm car."

I have said previously that I never pick up women. But I make an exception when a girl is with her boyfriend. Though I was a bit uncertain about their status, I felt that I was protected in taking the two of them aboard together.

"How far have you come?" I asked.

"Only from Billings this morning but from Denver yesterday and originally from Chicago. Last night we slept in our sleeping bags in a field outside a motel in Billings. We had a good night's sleep. Who would ever have dreamed that we would get caught this morning in a storm like this?"

"Had any breakfast?"

"Well, yes. We always carry a supply of raisins and raw carrots— the best food for hitchhiking. It's nourishing and doesn't get squashed up like other fruit and vegetables."

These two young people, though typical hippies in appearance, with dripping, shoulder-length hair and well-worn blue jeans, proved to be two of the most brilliant and fascinating traveling companions I have met in all my thousands of miles of driving.

They were both college students, extremely intelligent, and very articulate. He had just graduated from one of the most prestigious Ivy League colleges in the East, while she was about to enter her senior year at another widely known liberal arts college, also in the East. He had been born of Dutch parentage in Peru, where his father had been a mining engineer before returning to the Netherlands with the family. The girl's parents, on the other hand, lived in one of our major Midwest cities. Her father had been a religious journalist, but because his superiors had looked upon him with disfavor because of his too liberal views, he had given up that assignment and taken a position with a secular paper. She evidently admired her parents very much, particularly her father. "I'd like to be like my dad," she said.

Finally warmed and dried by the heater, both my passengers began to show signs of drowsiness and were soon fast asleep. This is true of many hitchhikers. After miles of trudging along the highway, sleeping on the hard ground at night, and often having to stand beside the road for long periods of time before getting a ride, they are tired. So I drove on in silence.

As we drew near a little town at the noon hour, I woke them up and suggested that we look for a place to eat. It was still raining hard, so I said, "I'd like you to be my guests."

The town was a rather dilapidated-looking little place, and we had to drive around a couple of blocks before we could find a decent-looking restaurant. We finally came to a dingy, old, red brick hotel with a faded sign that said, "Coffee Shop."

Parking the car a half block from the hotel, we dashed through the rain and entered the dining room off the hotel lobby. We were surprised to find it crowded with old people. It looked like a senior citizens' center. They all viewed us with curiosity as we looked for a vacant table. I probably could have been taken for a hippy myself.

Seated finally at a table, we ordered some hot soup, hamburgers, coffee, and apple pie, all of which proved to be well cooked, appetizing, and good. I enjoyed it very much, as did my young guests. "Certainly is great to feel full again," was the young man's enthusiastic comment.

I might add that I do not make it a general practice to feed the people who ride with me. The way prices have gone up on the hamburger circuit in recent years, I'd be broke before getting home again if I paid both for the food and the gasoline. But as in other things, I sometimes make exceptions.

During the afternoon I questioned them at some length about their manner of life.

"Isn't there a danger that in wandering around the country this way you might drift permanently into a gypsy style of life before you know it?" I asked.

"By no means," the girl beside me replied. (I'll call her Julia, though that was not her name.) "We have a definite goal in mind. My boyfriend here, Pieter, speaks Spanish fluently, having been born in Peru, and at college I have been majoring in Spanish. What we want to do is to go into the field of education, spending a couple of years first in teaching English either in Mexico or Peru and then going on from there. We are of the strong conviction that the educational system today is not meeting the needs of the time adequately. So we want to learn more about the real world outside the schools before we try to teach the next generation."

I pursued my inquiries further. "Tell me something about your religious views. What about the church? Do you feel that the churches are meeting the needs of people any better than the schools?"

"I happen to be a Catholic," she replied, "and I guess Pieter is, too." He corrected her. "Dutch Reformed," he said.

"Well, Catholic or Protestant, no matter," was her abrupt response. "We don't have much faith in the churches, whatever the name. We believe in God. But the churches are so divided and, like the schools, so out of touch with things that they don't seem to have any solution for the really big issues of the time—poverty, unemployment, family life, racial tensions, war and crime, and social injustice."

"Much of what you say is true," I said. "I happen to be a pacifist, as I have been ever since World War I. As you can well imagine, I have been bitterly disappointed in the silence of the churches regarding the issues of war and peace, at a time when they should have been taking the lead for world peace and the teachings of Jesus on nonviolence. It is incredible to me that people generally have such faith in military defense as a guarantee of national security. Actually, the fact that we are spending billions of dollars for military hardware is a threat to our security. The history of all the great empires from Egypt and Babylon and Greece and Rome right down to such European powers as Germany, France, Great Britain, and Italy in our own time demonstrates the fact that the people become so bogged down by the weight of military taxation that the national economy begins to fall apart from within. I am increasingly convinced that all that the Pentagon stands for is obsolete as far as national security is concerned."

Pieter and Julia shared my feelings completely. Nevertheless, I had to tell them that I did not take quite such a pessimistic view as they did about the failures of the church. The richest values of my life have come from the church—my family, my faith in God, my love of the Bible, and my hope of life everlasting. "Even though the churches are still badly divided," I went on to say, "my experience in the ecumenical movement indicates that the churches are getting to know one another and to work together as has not been true for a thousand years. In fact, I look upon the growing unity of the churches as the brightest sign of hope on the horizons of an otherwise darkened world."

My reference to pacifism opened up a burst of questions. Like most of the young people I have met along the road, Julia and Pieter were intensely opposed to the war in Vietnam. They wanted to know all about my trip to Southeast Asia with the Interfaith Peace Mission in 1965, in which Catholics, Protestants, and Jews took part. From this they went on to inquire about life after death, what my work was, and something about my family.

When I told them that my wife had died the preceding year, but that we had been blessed by three children, all happily married, they asked me to tell them more about what vocations my children were following. So I explained that my daughter, the oldest of the three, was the wife of an outstanding Baptist minister and active herself in many areas of church and community work. My oldest son, a Baptist minister, was now a professor of Old Testament studies in the department of religion at Smith College. In connection with this job he had been on several archaeological expeditions to the Holy Land. This excited their special interest, as did my report that my younger son, an M.D., and his wife, a graduate nurse, had been serving as medical missionaries among the mountain tribes in the jungles of northern Burma and Thailand. "Some family!" Pieter exclaimed. "Any grandchildren?" "Twelve," I replied.

All in all, the three of us had a grand day together. I would have enjoyed traveling farther with them. But as I was planning to spend the night in Missoula, they said they would like to try for another pickup in the hope of catching a ride to Seattle. It was with genuine regret that I bade good-bye to this stimulating couple.

There was an interesting sequel to this impromptu seminar on Interstate Highway 90. The following October I got a card from Julia, expressing appreciation for the ride and especially for our conversation on religion. I replied to her card in the same spirit. It was my boundless pleasure to receive a letter from her a year later in which she said, "Pieter and I are now way down in Mexico City, where we are both teaching English in Mexican schools. You'll be glad to know that we are now married and very happy. Pieter's my man!"

Ample reward for a bowl of soup, a couple of hamburgers, and some pieces of pie in that nameless little town up in Montana.

Among other college students I have met on the highways, I must mention one in particular.

He was a young black man standing by the side of the road in one of our northern states. As a student in one of the colleges in the next state to the south, he had hitchhiked up to the state university in the north for a weekend visit with his fiancée, who was a student on the campus there.

I was especially glad to have a member of the black race as my passenger. For one reason because it is more difficult for blacks to get a ride than it is for whites. Unfortunately they sometimes have to wait a long time. But I was glad, too, to have an opportunity to question a member of a minority race concerning his reactions to college life.

This young man had a very superior intellect, as well as a most friendly spirit. He was majoring in philosophy and hoped to go on to take graduate work. Although I did not think to ask him what he planned to do after getting his degree, I would judge that he was expecting to go into teaching. The late Paul Tillich, professor of philosophy and theology at Union Theological Seminary, was still living at the time and had lectured the previous year at the college where my newly acquired passenger was a student. The latter had been profoundly impressed by Tillich's theology, which was understandable, as Tillich was one of the most influential thinkers of the twentieth century, renowned the world around.

My field of study having been more in the realm of social action than in philosophy, I soon found myself involved in a conversation that was too deep for me. This young man was truly brilliant. Wherever he is today, I am sure he must be making an impact on all with whom he comes in contact. He was obviously a man of faith and character, with a keen sense of justice and a great respect for his parents, his church, and his professors. He was expecting to visit his father and mother before returning to college for the fall semester. It is heartening to know that from our American blacks, who have been oppressed and discriminated against for so long, there are emerging young people with such tremendous leadership potential.

A peculiar thing happened as we came to Interstate 90 where I had to turn east while he continued farther south on Route 75. When we arrived at the junction point, he opened the door; and, saying good-bye rather abruptly, he suddenly took something out of his pocket and slid it across the seat toward me. "Thanks a lot for the ride," he said. "I leave one of these for every driver who stops to pick me up." Before I could thank him, he was gone.

His gift proved to be a beautiful little paperweight made of a very solid, deep green glass in the shape of a sitting duck. Whether he had bought it or made it himself I do not know. Nor do I know whether it had any symbolism. Maybe it meant that any driver who picked up hitchhikers was a sitting duck for high risks. No, I do not believe that. I treasure my little duck as a token of genuine gratitude from a friend I may never see again.

3

"Belt Buckles West!"

Not all hitchhikers are young people. Some are well advanced in years, having spent a lifetime wandering over the highways of the nation. Nor are all the people waiting by the side of the road hitchhikers. There are stranded motorists, too—some of them with a flat tire or an overheated engine, and some of them who have simply run out of gas.

Two of these stalled motorists I found on Interstate 94 as I was coming into Mandan, North Dakota, from the west. Interstate 94 proved to be well named, for the elderly lady standing beside her car was herself ninety years of age. The car was ancient, with a mileage of over 100,000 miles.

As I pulled my car up in front of hers on the shoulder of the road, I could see that she was in real trouble. The hood of her car was up as a sign of distress, and the pavement was flooded with oil; in addition, some part of the motor had dropped down onto the pavement.

"Can I be of any help?" I inquired.

"Thank you," she said. "Help is already on the way and should be here soon from Mandan. Something has gone wrong with my car."

I was relieved to know that help was already on the way. When the Lord handed out talents for mechanical work, I must have been behind the door or something. I am a total disaster when it comes to handling tools, whether in a carpenter shop or a machine shop or in my own garage.

My curiosity was aroused when I saw another elderly lady in the front seat of the car, with her head leaning against the window opposite the driver's seat. Her eyes were closed as if she were ill or sleeping.

"That's my sister," the older woman explained when she saw the direction of my gaze. "She's only seventy-eight, but she has always been very frail. I'll be glad when I get her home again. We live in a little town just east of here and have just come from Rapid City, South Dakota, where they had that terrible flood the other night." I gasped with surprise. "You were in the Rapid City flood? How did you escape?" I asked.

"It was a narrow escape," she replied. "We had stopped in a little motel for the night and had just fallen asleep when I heard a pounding at the door and someone shouting, 'Run for your lives! The river's rising fast.' I got up in a hurry, only to find the water already up to my knees. As I opened the door, the man outside grabbed me and said, 'I'll help you get up the hill. It's our only hope.' 'Don't bother about me,' I yelled. 'I can make it on my own. Just help my sister; she's very feeble.' We made it to safety, and pretty soon a rescue party came and helped us to a refugee shelter for the night.

"The next morning they found our car about a mile down the river, lodged against a tree. I had it towed to a repair shop, and they dried it out and got it running again. But now it looks as though something serious might be the matter with it."

All this conversation had been something in the nature of a shouting match between this dauntless lady and myself. The wind must have been blowing forty miles an hour. When the wind blows in North Dakota, it's like facing a gale on the Atlantic Ocean. This fact greatly puzzled our daughter when she was a little girl only four years old. "How can the wind blow where there are no trees?" she asked us. A lack of trees, also, was typical of North Dakota.

I couldn't help complimenting the elderly lady on her courage in coming safely through all the perils of the week just past. Her sister had remained motionless throughout this entire conversation, leaning her head on a crumpled, old newspaper against the window. Expressing the hope that they might get home without too much difficulty and that the sister might suffer no ill effects from the journey, I bade the brave elderly driver good-bye and drove on.

As I thought of the way the two of us had tried to outshout the North Dakota wind, I could not help wondering what the drivers of the many cars whizzing by us would have thought if they had stopped to listen. They probably would have concluded that it was a senior citizens' convention.

Among the elderly people along the highway, there are hitchhikers as well as stranded motorists—men who have spent a life-time wandering from city to city. Some of the men I have picked up have been on the road since their boyhood. Frank Donaldson, a public relations representative of the Salvation Army in Phoenix, Arizona, where I live, described them in an address recently as a new breed of humanity: the American Nomads. They are not necessarily panhandlers, alcoholics, or job seekers. They are simply men who are incapable of settling down anywhere.

A certain type of nomadism has, of course, been a feature from the beginning of American life. Many of the frontiersmen, gold seekers, and fur traders were representative of this company of restless men. Robert Louis Stevenson must have had them in mind when he said that "to travel hopefully is a better thing than to arrive."[1] These nomads always cherish the hope that there is a pot of gold at the end of the rainbow—something better farther on.

I vividly remember how during my boyhood days on the farm in western Minnesota there were men called tramps or hoboes who often came to our doors for a bite to eat. My mother never turned them away, always inviting them to come into the kitchen and sit down for a cup of coffee, a sandwich, and sometimes a plateful of cookies.

There is a national hobo organization to this day, the elected king of which is known as "King of the Hoboes." Through the years hoboes have chalkmarked various signs and symbols on sidewalks or telephone poles across the continent, indicating whether the people living in a certain place would welcome them or sic the dog on them. A fine chain of restaurants today commemorates these men. A life-size statue of "Hobo Joe" and his friendly little dog stands in front of every Hobo Joe restaurant, welcoming the customers. Inside the dining room the walls are lined with the emblems of the various railway systems of the country on which the hoboes used to ride the rods. Pictures of "Hobo Joe" himself, sometimes shaving in front of a broken mirror and sometimes lying in a hammock and reading a copy of the *Wall Street Journal,* can also be seen on these walls.

The automobile and the means of swift transportation in modern times have greatly expanded the nomad's travel opportunities. Whereas the earlier nomads were limited pretty much to local areas, such as a state or a county, and traveled on foot for the most part, the hitchhikers of our generation can cover incredible distances on wheels in a matter of days or even of hours. They can cross not only state boundaries but national boundaries as well, all the way from Alaska to Mexico. Many of them are familiar with the entire continent. I have had some passengers who have felt at home not only in North America but also in South America and Europe.

[1] Robert Louis Stevenson, *Virginibus Puerisque: El Dorado,* as quoted by Burton Stevenson, *The Home Book of Quotations* (Binghamton, N.Y.: The Vail-Ballou Press, Inc., 1934), p. 2029.

An amusing example of such an elderly and widely traveled nomad was a man I picked up this past summer.

Returning from a coast-to-coast drive of over eight thousand miles—a three and one-half months' journey in which I had panhandled my way around a family circuit reaching all the way from Arizona and Idaho to Massachusetts, New York, Ohio, Colorado, New Mexico, and back again—I was approaching Flagstaff, Arizona, on Interstate 40 before turning south on Route 17 to Phoenix. This trip is a fairly good indication that I may be something of a nomad myself. And as an old man in my eighties, I am probably a fulfillment of the late L. P. Jacks's definition of an octogenarian as "a trespasser in the universe."[2]

A couple of miles east of Flagstaff, I was hailed by a rather weather-beaten man I judged to be in his late sixties or early seventies. Pulling up on the shoulder of the highway and opening the door, I said, "Where are you headed?"

"To Las Vegas, Nevada," was his reply.

"Well, I'm sorry," I said. "I'm going only two or three miles farther west on Route 40; I'm going to Phoenix."

"Oh, that's OK," he said cheerfully, shoving his tiny bundle through the door. "I'd just as soon go to Phoenix." (This would be only about three hundred miles out of his way—six hundred miles if he went first to Phoenix and later up to Las Vegas.)

So he got in, made himself comfortable, and then began a stream of conversation that continued all the way to Phoenix, with only occasional interruptions. He was a character—the most compulsive talker I have ever met and at the same time one of the most entertaining.

Pretty soon I was playing the part of chauffeur not just to one but to two characters, for as I was about to turn off Interstate 40 to Interstate 17 for the remaining 150 miles to Phoenix, I picked up another man about the same age as the first. No sooner had he got settled in the backseat than he said, "I met the Lord not long ago. I got three Bibles with me. Wouldn't believe it, wouldja! It's a fact." He must have met the Lord in a big way.

Here I was with two gaffers on my hands—both of them Irishmen. They had never met each other before, but they spoke the same language and were soon bosom friends. I didn't have to do much talking from Flagstaff to Phoenix. I could only listen. That was true pretty much of the time for the man in the backseat also. The old

[2] Lawrence Pearsall Jacks. *Confession of an Octogenarian* (New York: Macmillan, Inc., 1942), p. 249.

Irishman beside me in the front seat took over all the responsibility as far as conversation was concerned.

Suddenly he posed a question, "You know something?" One sensed immediately that an announcement of vast import was impending. In this conclusion I was not mistaken. "When I sleep out in a meadow someplace along the road at night," he continued, "I sometimes can't figure out which direction is east and which direction is west when I wake up in the morning. Ever had that experience? Especially when it is a cloudy day, and the sun ain't shining? But now I've developed a system so I can know. All I have to do is to take my belt off when I lie down for the night and put it down beside me so's the belt buckle is pointing west. That way I know which way is west in the morning. It works every time. Pretty good, huh?"

I had to admit he really had something. Belt buckles west! It was in a historic tradition. One time in the long ago it had been "Sails West!"; then, "Wagons West!"; later still, "Trains West!" So why not "Belt Buckles West!"

By this time my two passengers were on such friendly terms that one might have thought they had been two old cronies for a lifetime. They revealed an immense amount of practical wisdom that with all my college and seminary education I had never known before. They could identify all the flophouses, rescue missions, food stamp centers, and Salvation Army stations from Florida to California as well as up the coast to Seattle. They told me where I could get a breakfast of oatmeal alone or a breakfast of oatmeal with milk and sugar on it, too. They also warned me to be on guard against restaurants where I could get arrested if I went in without money and asked for something to eat, even if I offered to pay for it by washing dishes. All this information was handed out free, in the most agreeable and philosophic spirit, as if it were all an accepted fact of life. And I would not wish to be thought of as speaking too lightly about it. It actually is the way of life for untold multitudes of people, a large proportion of whom would give anything to be delivered from it.

Coming down from the cool temperatures of Flagstaff and the high country of northern Arizona to the 110 degree temperatures of the desert in the Valley of the Sun, we arrived in Phoenix about the middle of the afternoon. Because of the intense summer heat, I decided, much to their pleasure, not to let them out where I would normally turn eastward at the city limits but to continue on the Black Canyon Highway to the downtown area five miles farther on. "How about letting you off at the Light House Mission?" I suggested, knowing that they would be well taken care of there.

"Fine!" they replied. "That's a good place."

Following a brief prayer, I said good-bye to a pair of elderly Hibernians who I almost felt were my own buddies by this time. I wonder where they are now—maybe in San Diego, New Orleans, or Omaha. Who knows? Belt buckles west, north, east, or south I imagine would be all the same to them.

Several years ago I picked up another aging nomad. This was on Interstate 90, not far from Toledo, Ohio. I still remember him with some degree of affection, too. He was a sturdy Scotchman, seventy-two years of age, rather colorfully dressed in well-fitting clothes, with a red and white ski cap on his head, stout leather walking shoes on his feet, and red and white lumberjack socks to match the ski cap. A somewhat stubby, grizzled beard, neatly trimmed, added to his good appearance.

He told me he had been on his own practically all his life. He had been left an orphan at the age of eleven and had been hitting the road ever since. Through all those years he had wandered from place to place, getting temporary jobs wherever he might find them. He was a rather quiet, self-respecting man. He wanted to know if I had ever heard the Scotch song he hummed for me. It was Harry Lauder's old song "A-Roamin' in the Gloamin'." When I told him I had heard Lauder himself sing it on two different occasions, he was delighted beyond measure.

He was one more of those rare passengers I invited to have lunch with me, this time at a little diner along the road. While we were eating together, he wanted to know if I could draw a map that would show him where Scotland was. With the help of a paper napkin and a ball-point pen, I did my best to indicate where Scotland and the British Isles were in relation to the continent of Europe. Because he had had little opportunity to go to school as a boy, he seemed especially appreciative of this amateur geography lesson. Evidently his Scotch heritage had been impressed upon him rather deeply by his parents, whoever they were. He had been born in this country, however. For the first time in many years, he was now going back to his hometown, a tiny village just outside of Toledo, to see if there might be anyone there who would remember him.

Who knows what is in the heart of the lonely American nomad? A social worker from New Jersey said to a group of ministers in Buffalo, New York, some years ago, "The most persistent question of the orphan is, 'Who am I?'" The longing for identity and a sense of kinship are the basic instincts of the human soul. I was surprised only recently when in a group of ministers who meet for a prayer breakfast every Wednesday morning one of my closest friends said in a very personal prayer, "O God, I have never had a brother or a sister. You know how as an only child I used to long for that relationship. So I want to thank you for the men in this little circle, who are my brothers in Christ, and who give me the blessed feeling of a sibling affection."

This was the first time there had dawned on me the realization of what a priceless privilege had been mine in having had three wonderful brothers and two lovely sisters. I was the youngest and am now the only one left, all of the rest of them having gone home to that beautiful land which "by faith we can see from afar." So I can appreciate better than I once could the sense of solitariness in the soul of my friend who offered such a moving prayer at that Wednesday morning breakfast.

One of the joyous surprises of life is to discover the pure gold in the hearts of many men and women whose exterior appearance gives no inkling of such hidden treasure.

I recall an elderly man who came into my office one morning while I was pastor of the First Baptist Church of St. Paul, Minnesota. This historic church, founded in 1849, is located right on skid row, only two blocks from the rescue mission, an institution with which we had very warm cooperative relations. My eight-year pastorate there was during the Great Depression years, from 1931 to 1939. It was the common thing for alcoholics, panhandlers, and the unemployed to come to our church for aid. Probably 25 percent of our members were on welfare (a wholesome corrective to the popular idea that the only people on welfare are lazy good-for-nothings who don't want to work under any circumstances). It was almost impossible to find work anywhere. The mayor's welfare committee on which I was serving at the time was in agreement that while possibly 10 percent of those on welfare were chiselers who deliberately avoided work, the other 90 percent would have given anything for a chance to get a job. It is my opinion that those percentages are still true today.

Traveling across the continent in those days, one could see empty boxcars, flatcars and coal cars crowded with men riding the freight trains from place to place in search of employment. Railroad officials, realizing these men's desperate conditions, were fairly lenient with them. I think it was one of the most melancholy decades of the twentieth century (along with the winter of 1918–1919, when millions of people were dying all over the world in the great flu epidemic at the close of World War I).

This was the picture of the American economy on the morning

the elderly stranger referred to came into my office at the First Baptist Church of St. Paul. "Reverend," he said, using the term most people use in addressing a minister, but which ministers themselves don't like because it is incorrect, "could you lend me fifty cents so's I could go over to the Chinese laundry and get my clean shirt?"

I was pretty sure he didn't have a clean shirt at the laundry. He was in a sorry state generally, poorly clad and reeking with the smell of liquor. But I took him at his word. Then I said to Phil Zuniga, the young Mexican lay preacher who worked among the Mexican members of our congregation and who had himself come out of a pretty rough life before he became a Christian, "Phil, would you take this half-dollar and help John get over to the Chinese laundry? He says he has a clean shirt there."

Immediately John began to protest. "Oh, I won't need any help. I can make it over there on my own."

"Well, John," I said, "you look a little unsteady on your feet this morning. The traffic is pretty heavy around here, and I think it would be best if Phil went with you."

As they went out the door, our visitor still protesting, I had the feeling that they would soon be back. I was not mistaken. In a few minutes they returned, John looking very penitent and chagrined.

"Reverend," he said humbly, "can you ever forgive me? I never thought I would sink so low as to lie to a man of God. It was just that I've been sleeping on the park benches the last few nights and was burning up for a drink so bad this morning that I thought if I could only bum half a dollar off you, I could make it through the day."

"John," I said, "if you sincerely want forgiveness, I know God will forgive you. And if God forgives you, certainly I will. Suppose that you and Phil and I go in there to the study and tell the Lord all about it."

When the three of us were all in the study and I had closed the door to the outer office, I said, "Let me suggest that we all kneel down together here and pray. Phil, why don't you pray first? I'll follow you. And then, John, I want you to pray."

"No, Reverend, I can't do that," John objected. "I've never done any praying out loud in all my life, not when there was anybody around to hear me. Please, you do the praying for me, and let me listen."

"Don't worry about any fancy words," I said. "Just tell God what's in your heart."

Following the prayers of Phil and myself, there was a long silence. We waited patiently. Then John prayed. I shall never forget his prayer. "O God," he said, "you know how weak I am. And unless you help me, I'm sunk. Amen."

When we got up from our knees, I put out my hand and said, "John, if God ever heard a prayer in heaven, he heard that one. I'm sure that you will never touch a drop of liquor again."

"With God's help," he firmly replied, "I never will." And he never did. He lived a completely sober life as a total abstainer from that moment. In all my experience with many alcoholics, I have never had the joy of such an instantaneous and enduring conversion as his. It was a demonstrable new birth—convincing evidence of a man born again through the power of Jesus Christ.

The following Sunday Mrs. Dahlberg and I invited him out to the house to dinner after the morning service. He looked like a different man, clean shaven and neatly dressed. He had a keen sense of humor, and having been a successful traveling salesman before he became an alcoholic, he was a most interesting conversationalist. Our children were entranced with him as he kept us in stitches with his string of laughable stories about his own experiences.

When I gave the altar call that evening at the church service, inviting those who would like to come forward in confession of Jesus Christ as Lord and Savior to do so honestly and sincerely, John came. A few weeks later, after a period of instruction in the Christian life and faith, I baptized him. As he rose from the baptismal waters, his face was shining with joy. Not only did he become a faithful Christian and a dedicated member of the church, but also he became a member of the board of deacons and the Sunday school teacher of my own two boys. Because of his amazing conversion and his unusual platform ability, I often had him give his personal testimony at the Sunday evening services. His witness for Christ was so genuine and in such simple language that he always made a profound impression on those who heard him.

He consistently refused to accept any financial aid, being determined to make his own way. At first he earned enough to live on with snow-shoveling jobs and tending furnaces. Later he got a job as a night watchman in a factory. We all loved and admired John Eveland as an inspiration to us all.

Some years after I had left the church in St. Paul and become the pastor of the Delmar Baptist Church in St. Louis following a pastorate in the First Baptist Church of Syracuse, New York, I was invited back to St. Paul for the dedication of a new educational building and fellowship hall. This occasion took the form of a church banquet in the new fellowship hall. Way back in a far corner of the banquet hall, I could see John Eveland, handsomely dressed, his silver-gray hair and his rosy complexion making him a conspicuous figure among the many friends sitting with him at the table. At the close of the program he was the last one to come up and greet me. As he extended his hand, he said, "Pastor, I've always had a clean shirt ever since I met you." How we laughed together! It was the last time I ever saw him. But a year or two later in St. Louis I got a letter from him. It was a brief one but with a meaningful conclusion which moved me deeply. The last paragraph read as follows:

I am now over eighty years of age and may not have too much longer to live on this earth. But I just wanted to write to you once more, to tell you that I shall never cease to thank God for having led me to the First Baptist Church the day I yielded my life to him and accepted Jesus Christ as my Savior and Lord.

I don't think John was ever a hitchhiker. But he had been an American nomad until that day when he discovered the road of Him who said, "I am the way, the truth, and the life: no man cometh unto the Father, but by me" (John 14:6, KJV). From the day he struck out on that road, he knew the true direction of life. He needed no belt buckle west, north, east, or south. He knew the way that leads to the heart of God and was a nomad no longer.

4

The Millionaire Hitchhiker

While making an inquiry at the desk of the Phoenix public library one day concerning available books on hitchhiking and backpacking, I was approached rather hesitatingly by a young man who asked, "Did I hear you asking about books on hitchhiking?"

When I replied in the affirmative, he said, "I would like very much to have a chance to talk with you. Would you have the time?"

He was handsomely dressed, had an attractive personality, and was apparently a man of intelligence. As we went into an adjoining room where we could have more privacy, he introduced himself as "The Millionaire Hitchhiker."

Noticing my look of surprise, he went on to tell me his interesting story.

He had a good family background. His father was the owner of a small factory, and in her younger years his mother had been a successful ballet dancer. They had a family of ten children.

He was a high school graduate but had not been successful in graduating from college. He had gone from one college to another, six in all, without getting a degree. As he was telling me all this, I noticed that he stuttered badly. The serious handicap resulting from this impediment in his speech may have been a major factor in his frustrations—frustrations which led him to become a wanderer, living away from home.

When I asked him why he had introduced himself to me as "The Millionaire Hitchhiker," he said that at the time he began hitchhiking he had delusions of grandeur, engaging in fantasies concerning the glory and fame that eventually might come to him as a writer. In the course of our conversation, he revealed to me that these delusions had finally resulted in his commitment to a mental hospital. He had been discharged, however, and was now living in a rest home sponsored by a church mission.

I suggested to him that it might be a good idea for him to look into the possibility of registering for speech therapy at the University of Minnesota, which has one of the best speech clinics to be found anywhere in the country. If he could have his habit of stuttering corrected, it might help clear up the rest of his problems.

I was greatly drawn to this young man and hope that I may be able to follow up his situation as time goes on. Stopping by the library desk at the conclusion of our conversation, I asked the young woman there whether she could give me any further facts about the so-called "millionaire hitchhiker." She directed me to another woman who had been his hospital nurse. The latter confirmed the young man's story and said that his statements could always be counted on as being truthful. He himself had expressed to me his feeling that he was now back to reality.

This young man is an example of the unstable characters roaming the highways of America. Some of them may be so unbalanced as to be potentially dangerous. That is why the traveler on our interstate highways may see signs occasionally, "State Hospital," "State Prison," or "Do not pick up hitchhikers in this area." The point is well-taken and should be heeded.

In an earlier chapter I mentioned the fact that my hitchhiking passengers had been uniformly courteous and that I had never had any unpleasant experiences in picking them up. There was one occasion, however, when I had some moments of uneasiness. A rather heavyset, grim-looking man with closely cropped hair signaled me for a ride, and I took him in. He was so completely uncommunicative and shifty eyed that I began to wonder if he was an escaped convict. For self-protection I decided to pick up several more hitchhikers at the first opportunity. It was not long before I had three more guests in the back seat, all of them as sturdy and strong as a trio of secret service bodyguards.

Pretty soon there was a cheerful conversation going on among us except for the silent man beside me in the front seat. He continued to look nervously from one direction to another, never saying a word. When we stopped for lunch, I invited him to sit beside me in the booth and to let me pick up his check. How great was my embarrassment when he abruptly turned around and asked a lady behind us for a cigarette! She simply stared at him and said nothing. Being a nonsmoker, I had nothing to offer him except lunch, which he quickly consumed.

As all five of us got into the car again and went on our way, his silence continued. Suddenly he said, "I guess you can let me off at the next stop." It was not long until we came to a little town where without a word of farewell he got out and headed up the street.

"What was the matter with that guy?" asked one of the backseat riders after our strange fellow passenger was gone. Not one of us had the answer. We could only agree with the comment of one of the men who said, "He was an oddball for sure."

There are many people like him in our society today: loners who for reasons of their own are so silent and uncommunicative that they are puzzles to their own families and friends, to say nothing of the community at large. Most of them are harmless, good people, as dependable citizens as any of the rest of us. But some of them, though a small percentage, are in their inner beings seething volcanoes of hidden hate and fear which may at any moment erupt and result in berserk acts of violence that leave a trail of death and destruction through an entire neighborhood. The headlines in the papers almost every day tell the story of such tragedies: unexpected bursts of gunfire, murders, suicides, rape cases.

It will take more than police action to meet these situations. Police action will continue to be necessary, and we must give the officers of the law our strong support in their efforts to enforce the law. But I am constantly haunted these days by the words of the apostle Paul in Romans 8:3, "What the law . . . could not do." There is a point beyond which the law is helpless to effect any change in community life. Paul's whole argument in this famous but difficult eighth chapter of his letter to the Christians at Rome was aimed at helping them to see that only the spirit of life as revealed in Christ could deliver the human family from its bondage to sin, perplexity, and fear. We, as they, must look to God for the victory. "If God is for us who is against us? In all these things we are more than conquerors through him who loved us" (Romans 8:31, 37). Only as we put more of the spirit of Christ's love into the life around us can our society be redeemed from its present chaos, bewilderment, and disorder. Who is there among us who could not do more than we are now doing to put love, justice, and mercy into action?

The young man who introduced himself to me as "The Millionaire Hitchhiker" did not have a million dollars. That was perfectly obvious. Nor have any of the other hitchhikers I have picked up along the way had such vast fortunes. Their dreams of wealth and gold at the end of the rainbow have been mostly restless dreams and fantasies.

There is another large group of people whom I venture to include in the hitchhiking class even though they would vigorously deny any such affiliation. For the most part they may not be millionaires either. But they are rather affluent on the whole and possess much of the same spirit and philosophy as the hitchhikers, even though they pay their own ways. They are eager to see more of the world. They love to travel from place to place—sometimes with a specific goal, but often without any particular destination in mind. They usually travel in pairs or in groups of three or four. They are fond of a leisurely life rather than a working life. And no matter where they have been, they are generally ready to go somewhere else—but on wheels rather than on foot. They are a new class of American nomads, having appeared quite recently on the scene. I am referring to the owners of mobile homes, trailers, campers, and similar vehicles. Some of these wayfarers are young or middle-aged. But the majority of them are elderly people, retired people who have laid up sufficient reserves for their later years and are now looking forward to exploring some of the places they had neither the time nor money to see during their working years.

It would not be fair to put them into the same class with the hippies, the hoboes, and other vagrants and "thumbbodies." But in a very real sense, they are of a kindred spirit. Granting that these more elderly, retired people may have paid their own expenses and already made their contributions to society through the years, they have the same restless desire that the younger generation has, namely, to see what is on the other side of the horizon. There is something hidden behind the ranges which says to the questing spirit, "Go!"

It was probably this same yearning that led the parents and grandparents of many of us to leave their homes in Europe in the nineteenth century and come to America.

This spirit of adventure was a part of my own heritage. My grandparents on both sides of the family were already in their early fifties when they said good-bye to their ancestral homes in Sweden and came to this country, primarily for two reasons. They were looking for a better economic opportunity, and they were in search of religious freedom. Having become disillusioned with the state church—as is true of many of our young people who have become disillusioned even with our free American churches today—they broke with the state church system and became Baptists. As a consequence they were looked upon not only as heretics but also as traitors, since the church was closely identified with the state. The result was that Grandfather and Grandmother Dahlberg as well as Grandfather and Grandmother Ring were severely persecuted. My father, who was only twelve years old when the family left Sweden and became steerage passengers on a ship sailing across the Atlantic to the New World, often told me in his later years the story of how the police would break into their home and arrest the preachers. And my mother, who came from an adjoining province, used to tell me likewise about her older sister, my Aunt Annie, who became a Baptist at the age of eighteen, and who had to be baptized in the river at midnight, down under a bridge, to escape being stoned by the mobs that gathered. Fortunately those stormy days are a thing of the past, and a spirit of utmost goodwill now prevails among the Scandinavian churches.

On arrival in this country, my father's family almost literally became hitchhikers, though there was no way by which to thumb a ride. The railroad from New York to the Middle West ended at a little town in western Minnesota, called Willmar. Up to that point they were able to ship by freight all their belongings—clothing, bedding, tools, kitchenware, copper kettles, wash boilers, and everything else that they might need in a new and unknown land. All these precious possessions, contained in big wooden chests bound with iron, were stored in the baggage room of the Willmar depot. Then the whole family started out on foot for Ottertail County, 125 miles away, almost on the border of North Dakota.

Journeying through the woods and then across the swamps, lake lands, and prairies of western Minnesota, with no tents and burdened with hand luggage as well as blanket rolls, they were, in a sense, forerunners of the young Americans who backpack their way through Europe today, though the latter are bent more on travel adventures than on taking up a homestead.

Following the erection of a temporary shelter for the family at a little place called Dayton Hollow, not far south of Fergus Falls, Minnesota, where later all of us children were born, Grandfather Dahlberg got an ox cart and a yoke of oxen for the long, slow trip back to Willmar, with a view to picking up the household freight he had stored there. Great was his consternation when, arriving at Willmar, he found that the depot had burned down, with the result that all that they had brought with them from Sweden had gone up in smoke and ashes. Returning to Dayton Hollow with this disheartening news, he found Grandmother Dahlberg seriously ill with a condition that kept her bedridden for nearly the entire summer. The following winter brought additional hardship when in the severe Minnesota winter they were without adequate bedding or clothing.

But in spite of it all, they kept doggedly at their responsibilities. They organized a log-cabin church of twelve members a year before the now-beautiful city of Fergus Falls was founded, and developed what in time became one of the finest farms in Ottertail County. The church has today one of the most flourishing congregations in the community. It has an unusual number of young people present every Sunday and has sent Christian missionaries to mission fields both in Africa and Asia.

The hitchhikers today will do well to achieve as much. I have the faith to believe that many of them will. As we shall see in the next chapter, our modern nomads are not all drifters. A great many of them are jobless, looking for opportunities far away from their childhood homes. Unfortunately there are no homesteads available as in the cases of our earlier pioneers. But if they will put their trust in God and have as invincible a faith as their forefathers had, they, too, will win. The younger generation is made of essentially the same stuff as the generation that left other countries to come to America a century ago. Many are disillusioned with churches that lack spiritual vitality and that remain silent in the presence of injustices that would have outraged the Christ who wept over the city of Jerusalem and who had compassion upon the multitudes because they were as sheep without a shepherd.

Like the millions of young people, too, who came to this country from Europe to escape the military draft systems prevailing there in the middle of the nineteenth century, many of the hitchhikers of today hate war, having been entrapped in the same military draft systems that their fathers thought they had forever left behind. Like the homesteaders of old, many also have a yearning for the open country—clean air around them, blue skies above them, and unpolluted lakes and streams and fields. Rather than scorning and deriding the youth of our day, therefore, we would do well to know them, love them, and help them. Who knows? Someday they may make a rich contribution to our country—to its economy, to its freedom, to its religious faith.

5

The Job Seekers

Anyone whose memory goes back to the Great Depression days of the 1930s will recall the crowds of unemployed who could be seen riding across the continent on freight trains. I remember traveling from Minnesota to Colorado on several occasions with my wife and our three children, as during the vacation season we drove over dirt roads in our secondhand Dodge car to Denver for eagerly anticipated family reunions in the Colorado Rockies. While driving parallel to the railroad tracks from east to west, we saw literally hundreds of men riding the empty boxcars and flatcars as they journeyed westward in search of work.

They were the jobless men, victims of one of the darkest periods in the history of our national economy. It was a time when many of them had nothing to do but sit idly in poolrooms all day or play table tennis in the YMCA.

The personal tragedies in this situation were heartbreaking. Let one illustration suffice to describe them.

One morning I happened to call on a family that was going through unusual hardships. It was a large and good family, consisting of the father, the mother, and eight children. The father was not only without work, but was also suffering from a chronic and crippling rheumatic condition. Most of the family support became the responsibility of the mother and the oldest son, who was about twenty years old. They also received some minimum aid from the relief agencies of the city.

The above-mentioned son wanted to take his girl friend to the movies one evening. Desiring to make a good impression, he bought a new necktie for the occasion. This was before the days of blue jeans, patched trousers, and T-shirts. As a result of the necktie purchase, which amounted to only a dollar, a heated argument developed between the father and the son. "How in blazes are we going to keep this family going if you go spending a dollar for a crazy necktie?" cried the father in an explosion of rage and worry.

Utterly unaware of the family crisis, I chanced to come to the house at the very moment that this question was being fiercely debated. No sooner had I been briefed on the issue than it began to take on far more critical dimensions than just an argument about a necktie.

The son suddenly became furious. "All right!" he shouted, "if I can't even take some of my own money and buy a necktie when I'm going out on a date with my girl friend, we'll just pull out of this house, get married, and have a home of our own."

"That's what you think," his father replied. "Neither of you is of age. You can't get married without our consent."

"Oh, yes, we can," said his rebel son. "We'll just go down over the state line to Wisconsin, lie about our age, and get a marriage license without any help from you or anybody else."

By this time the dispute had gotten out of control. So I decided that as their pastor I should step into the picture.

"When I came to your house this morning, I came simply as your pastor, expecting to make a pastoral call," I said. "I had no idea that you were having all this trouble. But now that I am here, maybe I can help you find a solution to what is apparently quite a serious family problem. To begin with, suppose that we all calm down and try together to find the answer. OK?"

Things began to quiet down then, so I went on. "First of all," I said, "let's try to understand each other's position. We all know that these are pretty rough times for everybody—people out of work, worried about the future, and even wondering how they are going to scrape up enough money to buy groceries for today. So we have to try especially hard to be patient and to help one another."

Addressing myself first to the father, I reminded him of his own younger days. "Bob," I said, "do you remember the first time you went on a date with the girl who for all these years has been your wife? Do you remember how dearly you loved her and how anxious you were to look your best when she introduced you to her family and friends? That's probably the way your son Steve here feels when he goes out with Julie. I can understand how that dollar he spent for the necktie looks pretty big to you now that you are unable to go to work and support the family the way you used to. But after all, it was his dollar. He earned it himself. And when a young fellow is in love with a nice girl like Julie, maybe the necktie suddenly becomes more important to him than the dollar. Am I right?"

After a few moments of silence, the father grinned—a bit shamefacedly—and acknowledged that this was the way it probably was. So I then turned to Steve and said, "Now there is something I would like to say to you, Steve." Still rather sullen, the son nevertheless listened respectfully.

"Let me say to begin with that I think you are entitled to a lot of credit, Steve, for the way you have stuck by your father and mother, helping to support the family the way you have. I am sure they appreciate it, too, in spite of the argument you all got into this morning. So try to understand your father's position, even though it may seem unreasonable to you. He necessarily has to think about the rest of the family—your mother and your brothers and sisters—as well as about you in this time of financial anxiety. You are surely doing your part, but apparently it is not quite enough to pay all the bills. In a moment I am going to offer a suggestion for some added sources of income that might help pay those bills. Let's forget about the necktie and the dollar that it cost you. That's all a thing of the past. In the meantime, I hope you will not carry out your idea about you and Julie running away to Wisconsin and rushing into a hasty marriage. Getting married is a pretty big step. When that day comes, it will be a much happier day both for you and for Julie if you can have your family and friends with you, either here at home or at the church, and looking to God for his blessing. How about it?"

Considerably mollified by this time, Steve agreed that this would be the better way.

Knowing that they were already on relief to some degree, I said in conclusion, "Now let me talk with your social worker and ask her if it would not be possible to supplement what you are now getting." Turning to the father, I added, "I am quite sure, Bob, that in view of your present disability and the fine efforts that Steve has been making to support the family, there is a very good chance that your allotment can be increased a bit."

This promise seemed to lift the hopes of the whole family. The spirit of the entire group having changed for the better, I then asked them to join me in a brief prayer for God's help in the situation and that with his aid a new day might dawn for all the members of the family so that they might live happily together.

The next morning I met with the social worker, told her the whole story, worked out what seemed to be a reasonable supplement to the amount of relief the family had been getting previously. She was most understanding. Within a few days the additional allotment was granted.

This little drama had a happy ending. Within the following year Steve and Julie were married. Shortly before I left the city to take a pastorate in another part of the country, their first baby was born. One of my last acts as Steve's and Julie's pastor was to dedicate their baby son at the altar of the church.

I have taken the time to tell their story because it was typical of the anguish that thousands upon thousands of families in America went through during the Great Depression. The same tragedies are happening all over the nation again today, in the decade of the 1970s. Hard hit as the economy is in the present crisis of unemployment, inflation, and rising costs of living, we have been plunged once more into the desperate anxieties and tensions that cast a shadow over family after family in every state of the Union. Whether the jobless are riding the freight cars that rumbled over the continent during the Great Depression or looking for a ride on the interstate highways that constitute America's Jericho Road, these weary wanderers call for our most humane understanding and love.

We do not help the situation by dismissing them with such contemptuous generalities as "hippies," "no-good bums," "welfare chiselers," and "people who wouldn't take a job if it were handed to them on a silver platter."

I recall the sound insight that led the late Dr. Reuben E. Nelson, General Secretary of the Northern Baptist Council on Finance and Promotion, to ask the question, "How is it that the pastors of an earlier day, often without much education, and with no fancy buildings, pipe organs, or office secretaries, were able to win so many people to Christ while those of us in our generation who apparently have so many of these resources seem unable to convert the unsaved? I think it was because like my minister father they lived with their people, went out into the hayfields and pitched hay with their laymen, and often dug a little grave beneath the frozen prairie sod when the only child of a deacon and his wife died of diphtheria. All too often we are content to crack a joke in the pulpit about 'the lazy W.P.A. worker who leans on his shovel all day.' The joke may bring a laugh. But it doesn't bring any souls into the kingdom of our Lord."

Nor does it bring anyone to the Savior when we ride comfortably along in our smoothly running cars and say to the affluent friend in the seat beside us while passing a weary job seeker waiting beside the highway for a ride, "Another guy living off his food stamps while we taxpayers pay the bill."

And your friend grunts his assent as he replies, "Yeah—you said it!"

God have mercy upon us. And may he help us "to search out the cause of him whom I did not know."

Many of those jobless people deserve our sympathetic understanding—not only sympathetic but also active, helpful understanding. The least we can do is to give them a lift along the way. Many of them have no cars of their own. Or if they do have one, they may not have the funds for a repair job to get it running again. If we do not share our transportation with them, how are they ever going to find the job for which they are looking?

It is a humbling experience to draw forth the personal stories of some of these roadside strangers. Many of them are manual laborers, migrant workers, or farmhands. Occasionally one meets an office worker. During the summer of our American Bicentennial year in 1976, I picked up a certified accountant who had lost his job. His situation was particularly desperate as it seems much more difficult for a clerical worker to find employment than it is for someone who has learned a manual trade. This is not always true, however, as that same week I met a skilled plumber whose plight was the same as that of the unemployed accountant. It should be remembered that not too long ago a large number of highly trained scientists and engineers, some of them Ph.D.s who were the owners of $50,000 homes, were thrown out of work in the Pacific Northwest when the expected appropriations for big air force contracts failed to come through. Some of these men went inland for hundreds of miles, looking for a job of any kind, whether it be as a gas-station attendant or an apple picker. Nobody can be complacent about his or her economic security these days. In the twinkling of an eye, the most fortunate among us may find that the mortgages on our homes are about to be foreclosed or that we are standing in a long line waiting to get up to the window of an employment office for an interview.

It is true, of course, that a certain percentage of the hitchhikers are young people, either working their ways through college or simply skylarking around the country to see something of the world. I met some of the latter waiting beside the road on one occasion as I was driving down the beautiful Columbia River Highway in Oregon. When I pulled up to where they were standing, I thought there were only two of them. But suddenly two more stood up behind them, appearing as if from nowhere. This has often happened in my experience. These highway pilgrims, especially young people, develop a well-planned system of beguiling a driver into taking on more passengers than he has bargained for. Sometimes they partially conceal themselves by sitting down behind their partners. Or one of them will walk up the road a few hundred yards ahead of his buddy, and the man you picked up will say, "That guy just up the road has been traveling with me. Could you take him along, too?" It's hard to resist such a seemingly reasonable plea.

The four young people I picked up along the Columbia River Highway in Oregon that day worked this system on me. When I slowed down, there were apparently just two. One of them was a girl. All at once two other friends of theirs came scrambling up the bank to join them. They had very little baggage, so I took them all in. They were a merry crew—college students who had been earning a bit of money as cherry pickers. The cherry season having ended, they got jobs as apple pickers. They had proved too slow and inexperienced at this kind of work, however, so the boss had fired them. Now they were on their way home to northern California.

These young people provided me with an extra bonus. For one thing they called my attention to Multnomah Falls while we were on the way to Portland. This waterfall, tumbling down from the heights above, is surely one of the most glorious scenic wonders of Oregon. But set back some distance from the highway as it was, I had missed it completely on previous trips down the Columbia River Highway. We pulled up for the half-hour rest stop there, and my guests treated me to a glass of Seven Up and an ice-cream cone. Much refreshed we drove on, parting company at Portland, I felt well rewarded for having been their host for a few hours.

It sometimes happens that a couple of my passengers will offer to help each other find jobs. This was true of two young fellows riding with me into Colorado. One of them had a job laying railroad ties in the repairing of the roadbeds. The other had no work in sight. So the first one invited the second, a total stranger, to come with him in the hopes that he, too, could find a job with the same roadbed repair crew. A similar instance of one hitchhiker helping another was one of a pair I encountered on my way across Idaho to Seattle, Washington. One of the two was evidently a rather well-to-do young man who had been hitchhiking purely as a vacationer through Canada and was now on his way home. He was a college student with apparently some good business connections through his father's company. He mentioned a specific factory where he felt sure his newfound hitchhiker friend would find a job opening. Whether or not these promises ever proved valid, I do not know. But both instances illustrate the readiness of many of our American youth to help one another, even across the social lines that sometimes divide their elders. It is a fine quality.

To complete the picture of the job seekers who have been my passengers, something should be said about the more elderly men who, in many cases, have been seasonal workers and who have been all over the Western Hemisphere through the years.

One was a shrimp-boat fisherman I picked up one day during the summer of 1976. He was on his way from Florida to Oregon in the hope of getting employment on one of the Pacific Coast boats. While in Florida he had had the misfortune to suffer a bad fall that resulted in a broken ankle. After being hospitalized for a considerable period, he took on odd jobs for a while until he felt that his ankle was strong enough to warrant his hitting the road again.

"My family lives in Colorado," he said, "and between seasons on the shrimp boats, I always report back to my family. In this kind of work, I have to be absent from the family more than I like. But I manage to make a fairly good living."

He had worked the shrimp boats along the southern coast all the way from Florida, Louisiana, Mississippi, and Texas to the coast of South America. Now he was about to make a try for employment again off the western coast of the United States. He was a solidly built man, with something of a grizzled beard, and gave every evidence of character and worth.

He was concerned about the international controversies on fishing limits which almost brought on a shooting war between British and Icelandic fishermen in the Atlantic in 1977. The battle of countries favoring the 200-mile offshore limit, but restricted by the 12-mile practice, is a serious one. (The domestic legislation now being debated in our own country, which would require the tuna fishermen to guard against damage to the schools of porpoises that get caught in the same nets as the tunas, is another cause of anxiety to the owners of fishing fleets and their crews.) This situation should make clear the imperative necessity for the establishment of a strong international authority with the power to enact and enforce worldwide oceanic legislation relating not only to fishing rights but also to the oil, mineral, and agricultural wealth of the seven seas. The present economic wars between the nations as to who shall have the right to go in and grab all these resources constitute one of the most critical issues of our time. The situation as we have it now can result only in further chaos and anarchy, involving not only the possibility of the extinction of many species of life existing in the depths of the ocean, but also of the extinction of the human species as well. Something far more important than the jobs of shrimp-boat fishermen, important as they are, depends upon the outcome.

Ultimately we must be prepared to surrender some of our national sovereignty and join with all the nations of the world in some form of global cooperation comparable to the federal union we have now in the United States—a union that will protect the freedom of the individual units and at the same time guarantee cooperative action on the global level, with a world court, world law, and world police power to back it up.

The United Nations is one step in this direction. We must not abandon it. But the UN has no real power to enforce its pronouncements, other than world opinion which is often divided. Unless we face the issue of some measure of union that is international as well as national, we shall be plunged into the utter darkness of humankind's inability to govern the traffic either of the seas or of outer space. We need to think of all these possibilities of destruction or redemption as we pray the prayer of our Lord, saying, "Thy kingdom come, thy will be done, on earth as it is in heaven."

Regardless of the doubts, uncertainties, and fears prevailing now, an answer will be found if we look to God for the needed wisdom for the seemingly impossible tasks awaiting us. The apostle Paul said it well:

> I consider that the sufferings of this present time are not worth comparing with the glory that is to be revealed to us. For the creation waits with eager longing for the revealing of the sons of God; for the creation was subjected to futility, not of its own will but by the will of him who subjected it in hope; because the creation itself will be set free from the bondage to decay and obtain the glorious liberty of the children of God (Romans 8:18-21).

We shall need more than politics, economics, or other earthly measures to bring all this to pass. We need a sound biblical theology most of all.

6

The Lost

One of the supreme concerns of Jesus was for the lost. It was well summed up by his words as reported in the King James Version of Matthew 18:11, "For the Son of man is come to save that which was lost." In the Revised Standard Version of the Bible, this sentence is omitted in Matthew. But throughout the Gospels the emphasis is the same.

Especially is this true of the parables recorded in the fifteenth chapter of Luke:

> "What man of you, having a hundred sheep, if he has lost one of them, does not leave the ninety-nine in the wilderness, and go after the one which is lost, until he finds it? And when he has found it, he lays it on his shoulders, rejoicing. And when he comes home, he calls together his friends and his neighbors, saying to them, 'Rejoice with me, for I have found my sheep which was lost.' Just so, I tell you, there will be more joy in heaven over one sinner who repents than over ninety-nine righteous persons who need no repentance" (vv. 4-7).

The story of the prodigal son marks the climax of this immortal chapter in the teachings of Jesus. When the young man returned home to his father's house after having wasted his inheritance in reckless living in the big city, he was not sure how his father would receive him. But the father, seeing his son coming down the road, immediately shouted to the servants to get the tables ready for the most sumptuous feast in all their experience. "Let us eat and make merry for this my son was dead, and is alive again; he was lost, and is found" (Luke 15:23-24). When the hardworking older son of the forgiving father heard of his playboy brother's return and got wind of the celebration that was being put on for the black sheep of the family, he sullenly refused to come to the party. His father gently rebuked him. "Son, you are always with me, and all that is mine is yours. It was fitting to make merry and be glad, for this your brother was dead, and is alive; he was lost, and is found" (Luke 15:31-32). According to Jesus this spirit of compassion for the lost is also the spirit of the eternal God, our heavenly Father. This ought to remind us that one of the chief concerns of the Christian church should be to organize a competent "lost and found department." Still further, we must see to it that every member of the church becomes an active participant in it.

This was never more vividly brought home to me than by an experience I had one night in the Mojave Desert. Having made it a practice for many years to spend a night in prayer and meditation beneath the stars while on my summer vacation, I suddenly realized that I had never spent such a night in the desert. Filled with the desire to seek out a desert setting such as Jesus often turned to when he wanted to be alone with God, I started out from Los Angeles and headed northeast toward Barstow one beautiful summer afternoon. Finding myself in the desert well after dark, I followed the main highway until I reached a fairly good-looking road that branched off toward the southeast. A few miles down that road, I stopped the car and got out to test a spot just a few feet to one side where the ground might be solid enough to park for the night; I wanted to make sure that the car wheels wouldn't get stuck in the sand. Pulling off the road at that point, I parked the car, spread out a blanket, and prepared myself for a night of meditation and communion with my Maker.

Suddenly I saw the headlights of a car coming down the same road I had followed from the main highway. My first thought was to ask myself the question, "Where is there a place anywhere in America to be alone anymore?"

Slowly the lights came nearer as the car wound painfully up the slope in my direction. As it stopped alongside of me, the front door opened and revealed the unshaven, dust-covered face of the driver, who looked as if he might be a prospector.

Leaning out of the door, he called, "Are you lost?"

"No," I replied, "just camping here for the night."

"Well," he said, "that's good. This desert is a mighty bad place to be lost in." And with that he was on his way again. I followed the lights of his car with my eyes until they were lost behind the distant hills far on the other side of the valley.

It was beautiful beneath the open sky of the desert that night. But all that I could think of until the sunrise touched the eastern sky with the rose and gray of the morning was the concerned question of the man who stopped to ask, "Are you lost?"

As is true of the desert, the twentieth-century world is a bad place in which to be lost. And many are the people today who are completely lost—confused, bewildered, with no knowledge of who they are, where they came from, or where they are going. Among them are a considerable number of the hitchhikers I have met on the highways—nomads of the spirit, ever seeking for something they cannot find.

Typical of these wanderers was a young man in his twenties whom I picked up in western Minnesota, my old home territory. It was a stormy night, with a wild wind blowing and the rain washing the windshield. As my thoroughly drenched passenger entered the car and closed the door, he deposited the small bundle of his belongings on the floor and said with a sigh of relief, "What a night!"

As we fell into conversation, he went on to say, "This has been a wasted day. I came out here this morning, all the way from Minneapolis, hoping to find a job out here in the farming country, but without any luck. So I'm hoping to get back to Minneapolis tonight. You going that far?"

Unfortunately I had to tell him I was going only as far as Litchfield, the next town, where I hoped to visit some of my relatives the following day.

My hitchhiker friend fell silent. For a long time I found it difficult to draw him into even the most casual conversation. He seemed utterly discouraged. Finally he said, "Nothing I do ever seems to go right. I don't know what's the matter with me. Everything goes wrong. All I've got to show for my life is in that little bundle." He pointed to his wet belongings on the floor.

I couldn't help thinking of the day Jesus looked upon a crowd of hungry people in the desert and had compassion for them, for they were as sheep without a shepherd.

When we got to Litchfield, I stopped alongside an old established hotel where I had sometimes stopped for breakfast. Its prosperous days were over and it was now pretty much a home for rather elderly men without families. But it was still a respectable place. The rain was still coming down so hard that in all good conscience I felt I could not leave my despairing young friend adrift in the storm with no place to spend the night. So I asked him to wait in the car until we could work out some way by which he could have a place to sleep comfortably until morning. Although he had not asked for any financial aid, I provided him with enough money to get a room in the hotel just mentioned.

"Before we say good-bye," I said, "there is a question I would like to ask you. You said a while ago that nothing you ever do seems to go right. Do you ever look to God to help you when you feel that way? He will help, you know, if you trust him."

On an impulse I drew out my New Testament from my hip pocket and said, "I want to give this to you. You will find in this little book the whole story of Jesus—his teachings, his promises, and how he depended on God for everything. I read a chapter from this book every day; so you will find a number of passages that I have underlined because I found them helpful in living my own life when the going got hard."

He was reluctant to accept it. "I wouldn't want to take your own personal copy," he protested. But after we had prayed together—in silence at first and then audibly—he accepted it gratefully and promised to read it. Picking up the little bundle of his belongings, he said good-bye and entered the hotel. That was the last time I ever saw him.

One never knows the outcome of such an encounter. But as Jesus said, ". . . do good, and lend, expecting nothing in return" (Luke 6:35). It is the fashion today to look with scorn upon so-called "do-gooders." I have no ambition to be a do-gooder myself, especially the sentimental, busybody kind. But once in a while I like to take a chance on lending, expecting nothing in return.

One of the strangest examples of a lost wanderer was a young man on a northern Utah highway. He was only in his late teens. Since he was extremely uncommunicative, I bided my time before entering into conversation. Finally I said, "Where from?"

"Vienna," he replied.

Since he gave no evidence of a foreign accent, I questioned him further. "Vienna?" I asked. "What state?"

"Vienna's in Europe," he said.

I already knew that, but he stated this fact very firmly; so I went on. "Your parents living there?"

"Can't say," he responded very abruptly. "I don't know who my father and mother are."

This I could believe. Many hitchhikers are in that position. They are in the same class with the woman who wrote to the Mormon genealogical center in Salt Lake City saying, "Please tell me who I am." For as was stated by a social worker more than fifty years ago, "The basic question of the orphan is 'Who am I?'"

The person who asks this question may be an actual orphan whose parents died during his or her infancy. Or the one involved may be the child of unwed parents, left at some foundling institution or adoption agency. More often today these young people are orphans because of divorce—the chief sufferers from the many broken homes of our generation. This is by no means to imply that all divorced parents abandon or reject their offspring. Most husbands and wives who decide to bring their marriages to an end—often with good reason—love their children dearly and do everything in their power to avoid the unhappy consequences of a divided family life. Honor goes to the splendid young people who, though they have gone through the sorrows of a home where love had almost died, continue to love their fathers and mothers and, learning from that experience, have grown up to have successful marriages of their own. How many of them there are who have turned out to be exemplary citizens, faithful to Christ and the church. They are shining examples of the promise contained in the Scriptures, "When my father and my mother forsake me, then the Lord will take me up" (Psalm 27:10, KJV).

I have officiated at the second weddings of many divorced people. In almost every instance they have achieved complete success in their second marriage. As one young husband living happily with his second wife said to me, "I only wish I had met her first." Yet these same divorced people would agree that divorce is a tragic experience, costly to themselves and costly to their children. Nothing could be more important to society as a whole and especially to the Christian church than that by every resource of premarital counseling and by every resource of education, religious teaching, and community action there might be created that climate of faith, hope, and love by which a joyous family life might be the experience of every home.

During the course of my conversation with the young man I picked up in Utah, I gently said to him when he told me he did not know who his father and mother were, "That must be pretty rough." Then I reminded him of the words of the psalmist mentioned above, suggesting that he look to God for comfort and strength.

Far from accepting this counsel, he said, "But there is no God. I *know* there is no God."

"Oh, come on!" I exclaimed. "How can you be so sure there is no God? That's pretty hard to prove, isn't it?"

"I just know it—inside of me," he persisted. He was very firm about it.

There is no purpose in arguing against such a position. One can only bear witness to one's own experience. In a sense the young lad was right. Whether we believe in God or not depends on what is inside of us—our attitudes, our joys, our sorrows, our response to the world and the people around us.

So I simply told him about my own faith in God. I told him of the joy I got looking at the majesty of the mountains and the wonders of God's creation. I told him of the peace that comes into my heart as I think of how Jesus saw the love of the heavenly Father in every flower that grows in the fields and even in a flock of sparrows feasting on the grass seeds and the berries growing on the vines (see Matthew 6:26-33). Above all I spoke of how Jesus died on the cross for the two of us, and for us all, in his trust that we would respond to his love and, with the help of God, live good lives in the faith that when we die we shall enter into the resurrection with him.

As he listened, he seemed to be more thoughtful—less cynical. And after a farewell prayer, he thanked me as we parted company. I often wonder what the result of such a conversation will be. Will it bear any fruit? Only God knows the answer. In the meantime I remember that the ministry of Jesus was a wayside ministry made up largely of just such chance conversations. He gave his disciples instructions to follow the same procedure. When he sent the twelve on their mission to the various towns and villages around the Sea of Galilee, he said to them, "And as ye go, preach, saying, The kingdom of heaven is at hand" (Matthew 10:7, KJV).

We do not necessarily need a formal church pulpit for the proclamation of the gospel. Whether by ordained ministers or lay people, some of the best preaching today is probably being done as we go—walking down Main Street with a business associate, crossing a college campus with a student, strolling down a hospital corridor with a father and mother worried about the sick child they have just left in the children's ward, or guiding a blind person to the other side of the street when the green signal light says "Walk." Such simple things as these may be the means by which a lost and lonely human being is given the courage to enter the kingdom of heaven—for that kingdom is always at hand.

Probably the one hitchhiker encounter that has given me as much joy as any in my experience involved a young man who was charged with murder. I had not picked up this hitchhiker; I had just read about him.

While I was spending a vacation with my family one summer in Colorado, I saw a big headline in the *Denver Post* reporting that a schoolteacher and his girl friend had been found dead in their car in Wyoming one night after parking in what was popularly known as a lovers' lane canyon.

That same day a young hitchhiker who had violated his parole from an eastern state reformatory had come into Laramie, illegally wearing the uniform of an American soldier. This was during World War II. Entering a tailor shop within the city limits, he had asked the tailor to sew a corporal's stripes on to the uniform. Because he was a suspicious looking character already guilty of breaking the law in a distant state, the attention of the whole community was immediately focused on him. The town was in an angry mood. The young couple found in the canyon had been popular among the townspeople. Ominous talk of a lynching began circulating through the streets. No lynching took place, however; the police arrested the young man and took him to prison.

Although I did not know him, I was strangely moved as I read in the newspaper report that he had been booked for murder and that he came from the same city where I was serving as the pastor of one of the local churches at the time. Maybe I was subconsciously thinking of the words to which I have already referred, as found in Job 29:16, "I searched out the cause of him whom I did not know." At any rate I decided to take the train up to Wyoming and visit the prisoner in question.

Arriving the next day, I went over to the jail and got in touch with the warden. Introducing myself as a Baptist minister from the prisoner's hometown, I told the warden that I did not know the young man but that I was interested in the possibility of getting a lawyer to defend him. "Do you know of a good lawyer who might be interested enough in this prisoner to take his case without charge?" I asked.

The warden was most cooperative. He gave me the name of an attorney who had recently arrived in town from another state, after serving there with some distinction. "He is a very able man, but he is an alcoholic. If you can get to him while he is sober, I have an idea he would take the case even on those terms. He is that kind of a guy— always ready to help people."

The warden then took me up to the cell where the prisoner was confined and after introducing me to him, locked the door and left. This was not a new experience for me. I have visited in jails and prisons all the way from Sing Sing and Auburn to Attica and Tel Aviv.

The cell was not really a cell in the usual sense, but a fairly large room with barred windows. The prisoner was standing with his hands gripping the bars as he looked toward a distant mountain range in the west. The faraway peaks, crowned with new-fallen snow, were as beautiful as the promises of God.

As the unhappy inmate turned silently toward me, I saw a rather frail-looking youth whose face was full of despair. (In order that his identity may remain anonymous to the reader, I will use an assumed name for him in reporting our conversation.)

"Jim," I said, "I am a complete stranger to you; so I hope you will not think I am barging in on you with some ax of my own to grind. It happens that I am from your hometown back East; I am now on vacation in Denver with my family. When I read in the Denver papers the story of all that has occurred up here in Laramie, I thought I would come to Wyoming and see if I could help you in any way."

"I'm afraid there is no help for me," he said hopelessly. "It looks now as if I am headed for the gas chamber." (This was the state's method of execution.)

"Don't be too sure," I replied. "Things may go better than you think. Especially if you tell the truth, whether guilty or innocent. If you examine your heart in this situation and look to God for help, that help will surely come. Not only from him, but from others. I myself would like to do as much as I can."

As we sat down on the cot and entered into conversation, he told me his whole story—how he had been serving a sentence in the reformatory and had been released on parole. What he said about violating his parole by leaving his home state and heading west as a hitchhiker coincided with what I had read in the news report. He stoutly declared his innocence in regard to the murder charge. "I know I was foolish when I put on a soldier's uniform, but I thought I would be more sure of a ride that way. Why I asked that tailor to sew on a corporal's stripes, I can't figure out. It was a crazy thing to do. But I can tell you one thing, and this is God's truth, I did not commit that murder."

The more I listened to him, the more I believed him. As we talked together and then prayed together, he seemed much cheered, especially when I told him that there was some possibility I could get a lawyer to defend him.

Following this interview I returned to the warden's office to thank him for his courtesy and to get the address of the attorney whose name he had given me. Going over to the latter's office and having a long talk with him I found him to be all that the warden had told me he would be: a great-hearted person and obviously of high intelligence. "I'll be more than glad to take the young man's case. I believe as you do that he is innocent. People around here have been too quick to jump to wrong conclusions."

It may well be that this fine lawyer who had been a member of the legislature in another state before coming to Wyoming was an alcoholic. But I have found through my experience with many alcoholics throughout my ministry that they are in most cases basically good people: friendly, generous, and lovable—in much the same class as the publicans and sinners with whom Jesus mingled. Often it is their very friendliness and sociability that betrays them. They like the popularity that comes from ordering the drinks and saying, "This one's on me."

However that may be, this gifted attorney went right to work on Jim's case. Engaging a detective to help him, he instituted a thoroughgoing search of the canyon where the crime had taken place and found the gun that a ballistic study proved to have been the weapon involved in the murders. The fingerprints turned out to be not the fingerprints of the young hitchhiker but of a notorious convict who had been a prison escapee. Jim was completely cleared of the murder charge.

This did not mean that he was immediately set free; he had to return to the prison back East to serve for several more years because he had been found guilty of violating his parole. I visited him there on several occasions and through the years have kept up a correspondence with him.

There is an interesting sequel to this story. Following his release from prison, he got a job as a hospital orderly, was married, and had two little girls. Subsequently his wife died, leaving him with the two children for whom to care. One of them he brought up himself, and the other lived with her grandmother. He and the daughter living with him finally moved to a little town not far from his original home. I have not been able to follow up on the progress of the younger sister, but the older one has made good in a remarkable way. She became a fine Christian young woman, went to college, and is today a leader in the youth program of the church where I was pastor at the time her father got into trouble.

Two conclusions can be drawn from this hitchhiker's story. One is that the church needs a renewed emphasis on its traditional evangelistic function, which is to seek and save the lost. The other is that an equally imperative responsibility of the church is the developing of a social conscience in the collective life of the community.

Few men have combined these two biblical emphases more effectively than did the man I mentioned as having been my greatest teacher: Walter Rauschenbusch. On the one hand he exemplified in a unique degree a passionate concern for the redemption of society as a whole. As pastor of a German Baptist Church in what was known as "Hell's Kitchen" in New York City, he became convinced that the mission of the church required something more than the conversion of the individual. Out of his concern at this point, there came his lifelong labors for the social gospel. The publication of his book entitled *Christianity and the Social Crisis* brought him world renown almost overnight. Few books in the early twentieth century produced such a revolution in the thinking of the church as did this one, documenting on every page the sins of the social and economic order. It was a powerful and effective plea for the corporate salvation of society on the secular as well as the spiritual level.

At the same time he had a prayerful concern for the eternal salvation of the individual. I recall that on one occasion he paid the expenses of one of Billy Sunday's converts to come all the way from Syracuse to Rochester in order to give his testimony in our church history class. This man had been a professional safecracker. He had gone to Syracuse to rob a bank. Before committing his contemplated crime, he had drifted one evening into the tabernacle where Billy Sunday was conducting his vigorous evangelistic campaign. Convicted of his sinful life, the bank robber responded to the altar call, hit the sawdust trail, and yielded his life to God, thoroughly and completely. By this experience he was transformed into a godly man. His testimony in our church history class was history-making in itself. It made a profound impression on all of us theological students.

An even more eloquent evidence of Dr. Rauschenbusch's concern for the individual was revealed in a dramatic incident that took place just a few days after he and Mrs. Rauschenbusch were married. They had no sooner settled in their little apartment after returning from their honeymoon than a thief entered their home one evening while they were gone and stole all their wedding silverware.

Devastated by this discovery, they were relieved to receive a call from the police informing them a couple of days later that the intruder had been captured and the silverware recovered. He had pawned his loot, and the police had traced him by the pawn tickets. In response to this report, Rauschenbusch went down to the police headquarters to prefer charges.

Speaking of this experience to our class, however, he went on to say, "When I saw this poorly dressed man sitting handcuffed in his chair, looking so hopeless and forlorn, I didn't have the heart to prefer charges against him. So I went to the judge and asked if the man might be dismissed to my recognizance, with my promise to be responsible for him."

The judge granted this request, and the man was released to Rauschenbusch's custody. An evening or two later, Professor and Mrs. Rauschenbusch invited him to their apartment for dinner. Sitting at their table that night, the man ate his dinner, using the very same silver he had stolen from them a few days earlier. How like the story of the good bishop and the stolen candlesticks in Victor Hugo's *Les Miserables!* The robber became a good citizen.

During my last two years at the seminary, I had the good fortune to become Rauschenbusch's secretary, typing all of his extensive correspondence. The wide range of his human interests was revealed by the dictation he gave me in one particular week. Among other letters that week, there were four that especially stand out in my memory. One was to Lloyd George, who was the prime minister of Great Britain at that time. Another was to President Woodrow Wilson. Another was to a Sunday school teacher in a little church out in the Rocky Mountain area, who had written to ask for help in answering a question that had come up in her Sunday school class the preceding Sunday. The fourth letter was a letter of comfort to a little girl in Australia whose dog had died.

This concern for the individual was more than equaled by his concern for the social gospel. In this area most people would identify him by his great book, *Christianity and the Social Crisis.* It was published in 1907 and made him nationally and internationally famous overnight by reason of its ringing appeal to the churches to address themselves to the issues of poverty and wealth, war and peace, justice for the poor, and the need of radical change in the political and economic order. He would have agreed heartily with a statement of William Barclay in his commentary on the Gospel According to Luke, in which Barclay pointed out that the sympathy of Jesus was always accompanied by a sense of outrage, as on the day when he looked upon the hungry and helpless multitudes with compassion because they were as sheep without a shepherd.

Rauschenbusch's compassion was always accompanied by this sense of outrage, outrage at the all too frequent insensitivity of the privileged and the powerful to the sufferings of the poor. In spite of the twinkle in his eye and his kindly and unfailingly gentle spirit, he responded with a holy indignation wherever the wrongs of society seemed to be gaining the upper hand.

He dramatized these wrongs on one occasion by a simple action that was typical of his Christian compassion. Starting out at the threshold of his church, he counted all the curbstones over which a young mother would have to lift the wheels of her baby carriage before reaching a little park where there was enough grass on which children could romp and play. It was this sensitivity to the needs of his own neighborhood that endeared him to the people. He was always aware of the fact that saving the lost required two approaches: collective salvation and personal salvation, the redeeming of the community and the redeeming of the human soul. Only in this way do we have the total gospel. For evangelism without social action tends to be lacking in an ethical emphasis, and social action without evangelism depersonalizes religion to the point where it ends up with little more than a cold, ineffective legislative program.

The other conclusion urged upon us by the experiences recorded earlier in this chapter is that we should acquaint ourselves more fully with people we really, as a rule, do not know. The hitchhikers and the prison inmates I have described are illustrations. We call them hippies, hoboes, and what have you. But how much do we know about them as human beings? Like the Pharisees of Jesus' time, who were among the highly religious and respectable people of their day, we tend to associate complacently with a little circle of people much like ourselves. Consequently we lose contact with other people who belong to a different section of society. Our lives become narrow and impoverished as a result.

Job had hold of a great idea when he said, "I searched out the cause of him whom I did not know." He may have been patting himself on the back a little in his effort to justify himself in the sight of God. And if we pick up hitchhikers or visit prisoners and the poor, we may be tempted to pat ourselves on the back a bit, too, in the hope of attracting the attention of others. But personally I have had a great deal of enjoyment in getting acquainted with these hitchhikers and prison inmates. And I think I have in the process learned a good deal that I needed to know about human life. The chief reward, however, has been that in these experiences I have felt a nearness to Christ that I might otherwise never have known in quite the same way.

7

"I Hate This State!"

My rider and I were crossing Montana, headed for North Dakota and Minnesota. Vast in its extent, Montana is rightly called the Big Sky country. It is Big Sky country all the way from Missoula and Kalispell on the western border to Miles City, Glendive, and Glasgow in the east. This is the state that lifts the snowcapped peaks of the Rocky Mountains high into the blue, startling the traveler going west for the first time as he or she sees the mountains' distant glory against the sunset. This is the state, too, where the Gallatin, the Madison, and the Jefferson rivers come together at Three Forks to form the mighty Missouri River, which from that point goes rolling through the valleys and across the plains on its way to join the Mississippi at St. Louis. Famed as the scene of the Lewis and Clark expedition, rich in its resources of agriculture, mining, and lumbering, and beautiful in its setting, Montana is well named the Big Sky country.

I was greatly astonished, therefore, when the silent hitchhiker sitting beside me suddenly exclaimed, "I hate this state!"

I could hardly believe my ears. "You hate this state?" I asked in amazement. "What's wrong with it? I think this is one of the most beautiful states in the entire country."

"It's beautiful enough, sure. But I hate it just the same. People go by me in their big Cadillacs and point at me like I was some kind of an animal. Some smart young guys back there a ways made obscene gestures at me and laughed as they hollered, "Let's shoot him!"'

My young passenger, whom I had picked up just a few minutes earlier, was obviously seething with anger. And well he might have been. To be yelled at in that manner must have been pretty hard to take. Now he was transferring his rage at these scornful clowns to the whole state of Montana even though those who had yelled at him might not have been natives of Montana at all.

This is what happens when we treat one human being with contempt. All the more so when we vent our disdain and dislikes upon a whole group of people—another race, religion, or minority of any kind. The resulting hatreds, like a lighted match or cigarette tossed into a forest, may generate such a fire of destruction as to get completely out of control, leaping across all man-made barriers of law and tradition. When those fires die down, all that is left of an entire society may be a blackened area of smoldering ruins where the scorched soul of humanity is as desolate as the scorched earth itself.

Many hitchhikers have spoken to me of unhappy experiences such as the one I have described. I particularly remember a conversation with three young college men I had picked up one morning. During the course of our comments on hitchhiking experiences, I mentioned the fact that many of the older people of my generation are horrified when they discover that I pick up strangers along the highways.

"You don't know the half of it," said one of the youths in the backseat. "We hitchhikers are often more scared of the drivers who stop for us than you people are of us. We never know what kind of a person it is who is opening the door for us: an alcoholic, a high-speed artist, or some other crazy guy."

This was a new angle that I had not thought of before. The other boys agreed with him. One of them related an experience he had had while hitchhiking.

"One man stopped his car for me the other day and asked in a real hospitable way, 'Like a ride?' As I took hold of the door handle and had the door half open, what did this jerk do but step hard on the gas pedal and go roaring down the road at full speed! He nearly ripped my arm off. I don't know what was the matter with this nut— whether he was drunk, or panicked, or just thought he was being funny."

I could appreciate his view of certain types of dangerous drivers. Some of them are tailgaters, going fast to catch up with the car in front of them. When they are within a few feet of the rear bumper of that car, they continue to go at a dangerous speed, ever trying to push the driver in front of them to a still higher speed. Another example includes swivel-neck drivers, who, instead of keeping their eyes on the road, think they have to turn their heads toward the person beside them or even toward passengers in the backseat whenever they are trying to make an important point in the conversation. Then there is the gesticulator, who not only takes one hand off the wheel but sometimes both hands during the course of his or her eloquence.

Many other specimens of bad drivers could be mentioned, such as the weaver, who at a furious speed weaves in and out from one lane to another, snaking through the traffic in order to get to the next intersection and beat the red light. Worst of all the dangerous people on the road, however, are the drinking drivers—not drunken drivers, necessarily, but the social drinkers who think they are in complete control of themselves no matter how many beers or cocktails they may have had. The traffic statistics indicate that fully half of the fatalities on the highways are the result of the erratic conduct of this particular kind of driver.

Even those of us who are teetotalers, however, can hardly afford to be overconfident. Although I have been driving for sixty years without an accident, there have been times, nevertheless, when I have likewise been guilty of impulsive actions that could have resulted in tragedy. Only the grace of God has saved me in these situations.

Raymond Wilson, the widely known Quaker who is now the Executive Secretary Emeritus of the Friends Committee on National Legislation, has recently published his fine autobiography, *Thus Far on My Journey.* In it is one chapter entitled "Hitchhikers Are People, Too." This section of the book presents a poignant picture of the hitchhiker's side of the highway story.

"For more than forty years," says Dr. Wilson, "I have made a practice of picking up hitchhikers when I have room in my car. What a wide variety of stories I have listened to—such a kaleidoscope of human experiences. . . . My experience has been that on the whole, trusting people brings a positive response, and that having transportation to share has been a rewarding and enriching experience."

Driving up from Washington, D.C., to Haverford in the spring of 1974, Wilson picked up a young man on the north side of the Baltimore Beltway. This roadside stranger had been down in Florida trying to get ready to settle his young family there. While in Florida he received a telephone call from his father-in-law telling him that his wife and three-weeks-old twins had been killed in a truck accident on the highway in New Jersey. Shaken by this message the grief-stricken young husband started hitchhiking his way back to his home in the North.

Dr. Wilson was the ninth driver to pick him up on his long journey. But since Wilson was leaving the turnpike at Wilmington, Delaware, he stopped at the first restaurant they came to and began inquiring of a number of people whether they were going up the New Jersey Turnpike to his stricken and exhausted young passenger's destination. It took him nearly a half hour in that restaurant as one person after another turned him down. By that time even this persistent Quaker began to think that the milk of human kindness had pretty well curdled among the travelers he was meeting. This reluctance to aid another human in deep distress shocked him almost as much as the man's story. So they drove to the next restaurant.

There he found a man who at first hesitated, saying that his wife was very nervous. Dr. Wilson renewed his plea, telling the story as directly and vividly as he could. Finally the man agreed to meet the young man for whom Wilson was interceding. When Wilson introduced them to each other, however, the skeptical driver insisted on frisking his waiting passenger to be sure he wasn't carrying concealed weapons.

Commenting on this incident, Wilson went on to say, "Here was a young man who had gone through one of the greatest and seemingly most senseless tragedies which a man could go through, who would have to face the situation of a dead wife and twins in a couple of hours. . . . It makes one ask why some of us should be so fortunate as we have been when so many other people are faced with illness, or accidents, or tragedy week after week and month after month."

I thoroughly agree with Dr. Wilson's philosophy when he says concerning his practice of picking up hitchhikers for the past forty years, "I have never felt that I have really been taken advantage of or that my life has been in danger. With the amount of hijacking and gun-play and rising crime I would be a little more careful today, but on the whole I think it is better and safer to trust people than to fear them."

To illustrate his point, he concludes his chapter on "Hitchhikers Are People, Too" by reporting the experience of a professor who was running for congress in Indiana during a political campaign. The professor picked up a fellow one day who rode with him for a while. A day or two later, he got a postcard which said, "If you look under the backseat of your car, you will find a gun. When you picked me up I was desperate. I had made up my mind that the next person who picked me up, I was going to shoot and steal his car. But you treated me like a Christian gentleman and I decided to give up the racket."[1]

A beautiful example of what can happen in response to love and trust is found in the story of the sinning woman who came in from the streets to the house of Simon the Pharisee, where Jesus was the guest of honor at a banquet. This nameless woman, after anointing Jesus

[1] From the book by E. Raymond Wilson, *Thus Far on My Journey* (Richmond, Ind.: Friends United Press, 1976), pp. 201 ff.

with the ointment she had brought with her in an alabaster flask, kneeled at his feet, weeping. Bathing his feet with her tears and wiping them with her hair, she kissed his feet and anointed them with the ointment also. Sensing the fact that Simon was inwardly criticizing him for allowing such a woman even to touch him, Jesus rebuked his host. Calling attention to Simon's neglect of the simplest courtesies that a host would normally extend to his guests, Jesus by contrast reminded him of the lavishness of the woman's penitence, love, and devotion. Turning to the woman he said tenderly to her, "Your sins are forgiven." (See Luke 7:36-50.)

There has been much debate whether or not this woman and Mary Magdalene, from whom Jesus had cast out seven devils, were one and the same. Most commentators now believe this was not the case. But if they were one and the same, then Toyohiko Kagawa, the great Christian saint of Japan, was right when he said:

> If we are reluctant to accept sinners as our friends it means that we belong to the skeptics who deny the fact of the resurrection. Let us therefore remember that the first witness who saw the figure of Jesus on the morning of his resurrection had been a prostitute . . . The resurrection of Jesus was a resurrection for such miserable persons as she, for ruined souls.[2]

Little do we realize the degree to which we may drive the lonely and the despairing away from Christ and the church by reason of our judgmental attitudes toward the people whose habits of life are different from our own, who dress a bit differently, and whom we find difficult to accept.

What I have said in this chapter may seem to imply that it is only well-heeled automobile drivers who need to change attitudes toward hitchhikers and that hitchhikers have no responsibility in turn to change attitudes and ways of life.

Let me emphasize my strong conviction that hitchhikers, too, have obligations. For one thing, they are getting free rides. This privilege the average driver is willing to grant, particularly if the hitchhiker has a legitimate reason for being on the road. Such legitimate reasons, in my estimation, are these:

1. The search for work. If the hitchhiker is unable to get a job in his or her home area and has no way of going to some other part of the country to find one, common decency would suggest that the driver give the person a lift.

2. Going back to or coming home from college. Not every

[2] Toyohiko Kagawa, *Meditations,* trans. Jiro Takenaka (New York: Harper & Row, Publishers, 1950), p. 35.

college student can afford a car. His or her parents may not be able to provide transportation either. After having made all the sacrifices required by the costs of tuition and other expenses of an education these days, there may be little money left even for gasoline if the trip back to school is any considerable distance. I think the time will have to come when a college education is free to all just as a high school education is free today. In the meantime, most of us should be willing to share transportation costs with any family that has the ambition to provide college training for the children. This ambition was a religion with my own parents, even though my father never had more than an eighth grade education, and my mother had to leave school and go to work after finishing the third grade. By hard work on the farm, they managed to send all of us five brothers and sisters through college and a couple of us to graduate school. So I am perfectly willing to say to a hitchhiking college student, "Be my guest."

3. Emergencies such as those described by Dr. Wilson in his chapter, "Hitchhikers Are People, Too." These emergencies would include persons without funds who were called home for a funeral or some other crisis.

4. Soldiers and the aging. These two groups form a special class who are entitled to preferential treatment, as are the handicapped, who also are sometimes seen waiting beside the road.

On the other hand, a very large number of hitchhikers are less worthy of free transportation.

Among these are the drifters and the nomads who have adopted a lifelong practice of simply wandering from place to place without any goal. There will probably always be a great many of these—many of them lost, many of them lovable, and many of them derelicts—who are not likely to change their ways unless by some miracle they are truly born again. Society will have to handle their problems as best it can. In the meantime we must continue to love them and help them by our personal ministries in such ways as individually we are able to do so.

The chief obligation of the hitchhiker, regardless of background, should be to observe the ordinary courtesies normally observed as a guest in somebody's house. One of these courtesies it would seem to me to be is never to light a cigarette without asking whether it would be agreeable to the driver and to any others who might be in the car. Let me suggest in this connection that in asking the question, the smoker put it in some other form than the one so commonly used in restaurants, planes, and other public places, namely, "Do you mind if I smoke?"

I have never known how to answer this question. If the reply is "Yes, I do," it seems rather impolite and may result in a chill falling over the conversation. If, on the other hand, the answer is "No, I don't mind," one feels like a liar. Sometimes I think the best answer is to follow the suggestion made by one nonsmoker whose stock reply was, "No, I don't mind—providing you don't exhale." Spoken in a spirit of good humor, this may create a a climate of amusement, which should help.

In all honesty I must say that very few of the hitchhikers I have picked up have been guilty of smoking without first inquiring whether it would be annoying to me or to any others riding with me. My usual response is to say, "Well, I would appreciate it if you would wait until we get to the next rest stop. Cigarette smoke bothers my eyes a lot." And it really does; my eyes are extremely sensitive to the smoking of tobacco in any form, which is the main reason why I appreciate the increasing practice of the airlines, restaurants, stores, and other public places in providing nonsmoking areas for nonsmokers. This is a step long overdue.

We all have our prejudices, our likes, and our dislikes. The main point to remember is that we need to be considerate of one another. This is an attitude that should govern not only the actions of automobile drivers and hitchhikers along the highway, but also it should be prevalent in all the relationships of life, whether in the home, the church, the school, or in society as a whole. This attitude is what the apostle Paul had in mind when he said, "Be kindly affectioned one to another with brotherly love; in honour preferring one another" (Romans 12:10, KJV).

Robert Burns's oft-quoted poem sums it up well:

> "O wad some Power the giftie gie us
> To see oursel's as ithers see us!
> It wad frae monie a blunder free us,
> An' foolish notion."[3]

---

[3] Robert Burns, "To a Louse," *A Little Treasury of Great Poetry,* ed. Oscar Williams (New York: Charles Scribner's Sons, 1947), p. 563.

8

Flight from the Family

Family difficulties account for many hitchhikers' decisions to hit the road.

One of the most tragic examples I have ever encountered in this connection was that of a stock-car racer whom I picked up in one of our northern states.

As we entered into conversation, he told me that he had just been home for a few days to help his wife name their new baby. This was their third child.

"I'm leaving my wife," he said, "leaving her for good this time."

"What do you mean, leaving your wife?" I asked. "The mother of your baby and two other children?"

"That's right," he replied. "We can't agree about my work. She wants me to quit the racing game—says it's too dangerous."

"But hadn't you better think pretty seriously about that before you take such a radical step as walking out on her? After all, racing is a pretty dangerous way of making a living, if the pictures we see on television are any indication—cars on fire, crashing against the wall and all. What if something like that should happen to you, and your wife were left with three small children to take care of? Marriage and parenthood are pretty sacred obligations, you know."

Nothing I tried to say to him was of any avail. In spite of all my pleading, he remained adamant. "If I have to give up racing," he said, "life won't be worth living."

It was with profound sadness both for him and his wife that I said good-bye to him. Maybe he didn't know of any other way to earn a living. Evidently, too, the thrill of fierce competition for the honor, glory, and possibly the financial rewards that come with victory were the means of his finding fulfillment for his adventurous nature.

One of the most rewarding exchanges I have ever had with hitchhikers who had family problems involved both a very young man and a middle-aged man. I picked up both of them while driving through New Mexico, which is named on the state license plates as the Land of Enchantment. It seemed like a good setting for a highway seminar on love, romance, and marriage. The younger man, nineteen years of age, living in his own "land of enchantment," was in a hurry to get to San Francisco to marry his girl friend who was a dishwasher in the same restaurant where he was a busboy. The older man, apparently in his forties was in his own "land of disenchantment," having left his wife after a bitter quarrel about their three children. He sat in the backseat, grim and silent during the entire distance from Albuquerque to Gallup. It was not until later that I learned of his family problem.

As we rode along, I gave my attention chiefly to the young prospective bridegroom beside me, questioning him about his background, his plans for marriage, and something about the girl he was expecting to marry. He was a Southern Baptist from Texas but was inactive in his faith. He could not tell me much about the faith of his bride-to-be or about her family. But he was most enthusiastic about the wonderful girl who had accepted his proposal of marriage, as was befitting a true lover. He was a little vague about their combined income but was sure they would be able to make the grade financially. His chief concern seemed to be whether or not he would get to San Francisco in time for the wedding.

I suggested to him that if the wedding date had not been too firmly set, it might be well for them to delay it long enough to get better acquainted with each other, to put something aside for a rainy day, and to let their parents in on their plans.

"Above all," I said, "take God into partnership with you and commit your lives to Christ all over again. Start going to church together, and join some young married couples' Sunday school class where you can make friends and study the Bible together. A solid religious foundation in the building of a home is the most important consideration of all if a marriage is going to last."

My young listener paid respectful attention to what I said, thanked me for my advice, and promised to do his best. But he was still anxious to get to San Francisco. About that time we got into an immense traffic jam at the city limits of Gallup, the town known as the "Indian Capital of the World."

The annual intertribal gathering of Indians from all over the continent was just coming to its conclusion that weekend. The bumper-to-bumper traffic line had been at a standstill for the better part of an hour when suddenly the young lad bound for San

Francisco said, "I think it would be a good idea for me to get out here and walk up to the head of the line while all these cars are standing still. I'd like to get going! Maybe I can catch a ride quicker by going up front."

Bidding me good-bye, he opened the door and was gone. Whether or not my admonitions will have any effect on his marriage, I will never know. It is no doubt true that as a marriage counselor said on one occasion concerning his own marriage counseling, "They'll probably get married anyway." On the other hand, I recall a young husband who came into my study a few years after he and his wife were married. He said, "Pastor, at the time you were counseling us before the wedding, I didn't always pay too much attention to what you were saying. But as little misunderstandings have come up between us since then, I have often said to my wife, 'Honey, this is just what the preacher was telling us!' Then we have had a good laugh together. It's been a big help."

I invited my silent backseat passenger to be my guest at lunch. The traffic line had moved along far enough by that time so that we were right up to a restaurant parking lot.

He seemed glad to accept. Following the giving of our order and the arrival of a cup of hot coffee for each of us, he relaxed and began to tell his story while we were waiting for our food to be brought.

"Maybe you noticed that back there in the rear of your car I had nothing to say all morning," he said. "But I was listening to everything you were saying to that young fellow beside you. You were absolutely right in what you were telling him—especially about the importance of religious faith, patience, and love. I hope he takes it to heart."

"So do I. He may have to learn it the hard way," I replied. "But who knows? That busboy and his dishwasher girl friend may have a beautiful marriage—better than a lot of people whose situation looks more promising. Now tell me something about yourself. Do you have a family?"

He hesitated a moment. Then he opened up, slowly at first. "I'm kind of ashamed to tell you," he began. "The truth is, we are right in the middle of a family crisis. A couple of weeks ago, my wife and I got into a big argument one evening. We have three children. They are all good kids, but I have a hot temper, and one night they got on my nerves. I cracked down on them pretty hard—harder than I should have, I guess. My wife began to jump on me for being so tough on the youngsters; and before we knew it, one word led to another until things got completely out of control. By that time my wife was in tears. So I just got some of my things together and, without another word, walked out on her. I haven't seen her since."

He seemed unable to go on. He was obviously in great anguish. I waited quietly until he got control of his emotions.

"What has happened in the meantime?" I asked.

"I went home to Kansas to see my folks, hitchhiking all the way. The two weeks I spent there gave me time to do some serious thinking. Now I am on my way back to California. I'm going to go back to my wife and ask her to forgive me. She was right and I was wrong. She is a good woman, and our three children are as fine as they make 'em. With God's help I'm going to try to be a better man—a good husband and a good father."

It was plain to me that he was truly penitent. I encouraged him to believe in himself and to trust in Jesus Christ as his Savior. I reminded him of the promise of the Bible that "as many as received him, to them gave he power to become the sons of God" (John 1:12, KJV).

Most of the customers having finished their lunch and left the restaurant by this time, we were pretty much by ourselves at our table. So having wished him well, I asked him to bow with me in prayer. It was a brief prayer. I simply asked God to bless him and to help both his wife and him to win a Christian victory for themselves and for their children.

We then said good-bye to each other, as I was planning to stay in Gallup for the rest of the day and for the night as well. My noon hour with this penitent man was one of the best experiences I have had with any of my hitchhiker friends.

I received something of a bonus as a result of my layover in Gallup. For many years my wife and I had gone through that interesting community in the hope of seeing the Indian celebration. But we had always come home from our vacations too early or too late for it. This time I was determined to attend. So after getting a motel reservation, I turned my car toward the little sports stadium where the program was being held. So great was the throng of Indians and tourists, however, that I had to park a mile from the grounds and walk the rest of the way. By this time the stands were so crowded that I couldn't even buy a ticket for standing room. I tried every gate without success. One tourist who had purchased tickets months earlier for himself and his family couldn't get in even with the tickets. The man had come all the way from Vermont and was much upset, as he had reason to be. They did refund his money, however.

Just as I was turning away, greatly disappointed, two little Indian boys standing by me said eagerly, "There's a hole in the fence where we think you can get in. Come on—we'll show you!" I followed them just as eagerly. Sure enough, there was the hole in the fence. As I put my hand into my pocket to give them a tip, they ran away as fast as they had come. Evidently they were not looking for any other reward than having done their good deed for the day. Was I ever grateful for those two Indian lads! The hole in the fence was something of a tight squeeze, but I made it and saw the whole program for free. And it was a marvelous program, with the roping of bulls and with thrilling Indian sports events. Not only did United States tribes participate but also tribes from as far away as Mexico and South America took part in this celebration. I hope there will be at least a hole in the fence when I get up to heaven! And that the two Indian boys will be there.

Returning to the family and to its tensions, particularly as revealed by my hitchhiker friends through the years, let me give just one more illustration. I did not, in this instance, personally meet the hitchhiker, as I was not on the road at the time. The story was revealed to me by his heartbroken grandparents who came to me for counsel. It involved their grandson and their son.

The father was a military officer serving as a career man in the army. Accustomed to strict military discipline, he imposed something of the same strict discipline on his son. At last the boy rebelled and ran away from home.

For many weeks there was no word from him. The police were trying to locate him, but, busy as they are with thousands of similar cases, it was like finding a needle in a haystack. The family was desperate with anxiety.

Finally the police located the young man in a distant state, where he was visiting his girl friend. The girl's father put in a long-distance call to the father of the boy, but the father of the teenage son was so angry with the lad that he refused to receive the call.

This was where the military-minded father made his major mistake. It was a blunder that complicated the whole situation. The grandparents, reporting to me what had happened, were distressed beyond measure. There was little that either they or I could do, all of us being more than a thousand miles away from the scene where all this was taking place. The best I could do for them by way of comfort was to pray with them. Fortunately the son returned home some time later, and, so far as I know up to this point, things are back to normal in the relationship between the son and his father.

The American family today is in real trouble. The trouble reaches out in every direction. It is exemplified in the tensions between husbands and wives, parents and children, brothers and sisters. It seems almost as if the family were in flight from itself, trying to get away from all of its problems and tension.

There are many reasons for what is happening. The state of our economy has much to do with it. People who are out of work and worried to the point where they wonder how they are to put food on the table for their children the next day often become desperate. They rail at one another, try to fix the blame on one another, until the whole situation bogs down. Some run away, abandoning the home. Some turn to another mate, to another religion, or to another part of the country, always thinking they will find something better over the rainbow. But rarely do they find it.

Wars have also contributed to the breakup of family life. Long absences of lovers, husbands, and wives from each other; exposure to strange cultures in distant lands; homesickness, loneliness, temptation, infidelity, children born out of wedlock, alcoholism, drug addiction, death, and despair—all these inevitably lead to a massive upheaval in vast areas of the traditional family relationships. All honor goes to that great majority of men and women who, surviving all this, return from the wars as fine as they went away and live to establish the kinds of homes that help the nation to endure.

The mass media, too, as represented by television, the press, and the type of love songs, entertainment, and sex-oriented advertising that downgrades everything that once was considered holy, must take much of the blame for existing conditions. We are inclined too often to lay the blame on the home itself, particularly accusing fathers and mothers as being chiefly at fault. But even with the best that they can do, it is difficult for them to counteract the impact of all that is pouring in on the family from the surrounding environment. As Plutarch said nearly two thousand years ago, "Golden parents often have leaden children, and leaden parents often have golden children."

The analyses of the causes of family breakdown could go on forever. We could point the finger of scorn and accusation in many directions—at the church, at the schools, at the government, and many other institutions of our society. But what is needed most is not more surveys and "studies in depth" of the causes of the present state of affairs. What we really need is to find someone who will come forth with the answers.

I know it sounds very simple to say that Christ is the answer and to put a bumper sticker on the back of the family car advertising the slogan, "I FOUND IT!" It is not all that simple. But we had better think about it. There is a tragic spiritual vacuum, an emptiness, a longing for the Eternal, at the heart of our family life. Unless we fill that vacuum with a living faith, a thousand demonic forces will rush in to fill it with evils fearful to contemplate. As Hitler said of his rise to power, "I saw empty thrones everywhere. I simply went in and sat down on one of them."

If God is not on the throne of the home, if there is no prayer, no church relationship, no Christian education, if there is a complete ignorance of the Bible and of the spiritual heritage of the race, then the Prince of Darkness will come in to fill the vacuum. The final result will inevitably be total disaster.

Thousands upon thousands of homes can bear witness that where the light of Christ has come, there is abundance of life and joy, with a new sense of responsibility for each individual, for the nation and the world.

Many years ago I ran across a statement the source of which I cannot remember. The author of it said, "When I was a child I was governed not so much by the authority of my parents as by the authority to which I saw them looking up." That was the story of my childhood, too. God—the God revealed by Jesus Christ, a God of love and peace and joy—was the final authority for conscience and for conduct. Where there is that authority ruling over the home, every member of the family has a point of reference by which to be guided. I am thankful that it was my privilege to have that kind of a home. Unfortunately many of the hitchhikers I have met along the highways of our country have not enjoyed that kind of home. That may be one reason they are in flight from it. They will probably never find peace and rest until they find their home in God.

It is a sign of hope that a considerable number of these hitchhikers are earnestly seeking that heavenly home. In the state of Washington I saw a young person apparently of high school age sitting quietly on a rock beside the road and reading his Bible. On another occasion I was driving along a country road quite early in the morning, on my way back to the interstate highway through Colorado. As I turned from the little traveled country road to go up the ramp to the main highway, I stopped for a young man sitting on his backpack, seemingly in meditation.

When he had gotten into the car, I asked, "How long have you been waiting? There's not very much traffic on this road."

"That's true," he replied. "I've been waiting for nearly two hours. But the time passed quickly. I have been thinking about God and the beauty of the world he has made—the sunrise, the birds singing, and the mystery of everything."

Later in the morning we picked up two college students from Switzerland. They had come to Canada to see the Olympic games and then to the United States to see the Bicentennial celebrations. Now they were hitchhiking through the country to see more of America before returning home.

Instantly there was a fine rapport established between them and the young man I had picked up earlier, who was also a college student. They had much in common. By a rather unusual coincidence, we came to a little town during the noon hour where we found a delightful Swiss restaurant. Sharing our food together and discussing our various interests and experiences as we sat at a table together, we had a most enjoyable lunch hour.

Before the Swiss students had joined us earlier in the day, the young American hitchhiker had told me a good deal about his background. His mother was divorced, and he apparently did not know very much about his father—where or who his father was. But he greatly loved and admired his mother and wanted very much to have his newfound Swiss friends meet her. "There's an extra room at our house. Come and spend the night there. It won't cost you anything."

The boys from Switzerland were at first somewhat doubtful about accepting his invitation, evidently feeling that they might be imposing. But the young man continued to urge them. "Come on," he said. "You should see the inside of an American home before you go back. I live only about a hundred miles south of here, and we can easily make it before dark." This line of reasoning seemed to appeal to them. So much to the pleasure of their would-be host, they agreed. A few miles farther up the highway they bade me good-bye and went on their way, a happy trio.

In young people like this, I believe we can see the promise of a spiritual revival in America. Granting that they are a happy-go-lucky, carefree lot, they have one great quality much needed in the world today, especially in the circles of the Christian church. They are adventurous, little concerned about money or worldly success, and they love people, especially the poor and the homeless. True, they wear patched jeans that are ragged at the edges and pretend a kind of phony poverty. As one mother said to me about her hippie-looking son, "He looks like a ski bum." But this is a passing fad, little more than a sign of rebellion. There are already some signs of a return to elegance, a state of mind much to be desired. Many parents would agree with the statement Dr. Gene Bartlett made when speaking before the American Baptist Convention as its president some years ago, "As it is now when we look at our children, it is sometimes difficult to know whether we are looking at our descendants or our ancestors."

If we are pessimistic about the trends of modern youth, we would do well to remember St. Francis of Assisi, the immortal Italian monk whose ministry to the poor and to the lepers more than seven hundred years ago is enshrined forever in the memory of the Christian church. While in his youth he was by no means a saint. On the contrary, he was the leader in all the wildest escapades of the time.[1] As the son of one of the wealthiest merchants in the town, he was at one time crowned by his friends as the king of the revelers, following a banquet he himself had given them. Often these reckless young men would race through the streets at midnight on horseback, like so many hot-rodders, hurling their empty wine jugs through house windows, startling citizens as they went galloping on their way through the night. Yet it was this young "king of the revelers" whom God chose to be the most Christlike saint of the ages. Sickened by the affluence of his home and the godlessness of his companions, he rejected all his family's wealth, divested himself of his fashionable clothes, and went forth to preach the gospel to the lepers, the outcasts, the thieves and beggars that roamed the town, as well as to the rich. In his love of everything that God had made, he communed with nature, too, listening to the birds and making friends with the four-footed little creatures of the woods as he meditated upon the sufferings of Christ upon the cross. Who can say that it is outside the realm of possibility for the eternal God to be working even now in the heart of some rebel youth on the highways of America whom He has chosen to chasten and cleanse the soul of our own generation?

Spiritual renewal happened in the heart of another Italian youth in the fifteenth century, shortly before the discovery of America by Christopher Columbus. His name was Girolamo Savonarola, born at Ferrara on September 21, 1452. Like St. Francis, Savonarola was born into a home of considerable affluence and privilege, actually a courtier's household. But he felt nothing but contempt for court life. Full of doubt and self-distrust at the age of twenty-two, his doubts were dispelled by a sermon he heard at Faenza. How those of us who are pastors and preachers should become more aware of the transformation that can be brought about in the life of even one of our hearers by the preaching of a powerful sermon! Savonarola entered the Dominican order at Bologna forthwith and spent six

[1] *Encyclopaedia Britannica* (Published in 1945 by Encyclopaedia Britannica Ltd. Copyright in the United States of America), vol. 9, pp. 672-673.

years in training there before undertaking his first preaching mission. At first he had few hearers, but it was not long before he gained such power in his preaching by reason of his warnings of the wrath to come as well as by the tender pathos of his divine mercy that he was invited to become the preacher at St. Mark's Cathedral.

He had a special appeal to the children and the youth of the city. The same young hoodlums who previously had vandalized the gardens and public buildings, beaten citizens in the streets after dark, and become a threat to the whole community were so changed by Savonarola's messages that within a few months these same young people were marching through the streets in white robes and singing the hymns of the church. Pleasure-loving Florence rejected its pomps and its vanities, so complete was the transformation.

Eloquent preacher and reformer that he was, Savonarola denounced the corruptions of the church and challenged the tyranny of popes, priests, and the political leaders of the state to the point where they turned against him in such a fury of hostility that even his followers began to desert him.

Sentenced to death and tortured beyond belief, he was executed between two of his disciples who were hung from the arms of a cross before he was hung on the center beam. Then the cross was set on fire and the remains thrown into the River Arno at dusk. Every year on the anniversary of Savonarola's death, flowers are placed on the spot where it took place. A martyr to his faith, Savonarola became in a very real sense an advance herald of Martin Luther's Protestant Reformation.[2]

Someone may say, "What has all this to do with hitchhikers?" Simply this: In many respects the lives of St. Francis and Savonarola both had their beginnings in conditions similar to those from which many of our hitchhikers come. St. Francis and Savonarola were rebels against the luxury and affluence of their homes. They rejected the plans and dreams their parents had for their future. They questioned the values of the church and society. They were lovers of nature and, in a sense, troubadours of the Spirit, clothed sometimes in rags and wandering over the earth like beggars. Not all of our hitchhikers today represent the values of St. Francis and Savonarola, but some of them do. May it not be that in the grace of God there may be among them the preachers, reformers, and saints of the church who shall be the leaders of the coming revival?

All that is needed for such a revival, according to a book written

---

[2] *Encyclopaedia Britannica,* edition for 1968, s.v. Savonarola, Girolamo.

by James Burns of Great Britain entitled *Revivals: Their Laws and Leaders,* is that three conditions be present in the surrounding society:

1. A growing discontent in people's hearts at the prevailing corruption and backsliding.
2. An intense desire for better things.
3. A growing spirit of expectancy in many that a change is at hand.[3]

All these conditions are now present in our society. But as James Burns said in this book:

> Revivals cannot be predicted. Their movements are mysterious and incalculable. Revivals appear "in the fulness of the times," when preparation has been made for them, when the times are ripe, and when the heart of man is ready for them. . . . At last, when all the contributing streams which have been converging toward a definite point meet in answer to a definite and imperious demand, there suddenly appears the prophet, the messenger, who with an authentic voice speaks for God and whose accents men instantly recognize and obey.[4]

These conditions—the growing discontent, the intense desire for better things, and the growing spirit of expectancy in many that a change is at hand—are evident in every section of the society around us. Only one thing is lacking: the prophet, the messenger, who with an authentic voice speaks for God and whose accents men and women in every area of our culture will instantly recognize and obey.

Who will go for us? No one can precisely identify that person as yet. Maybe it will be some farm boy or girl from the rural areas of our country. Maybe it will be some poverty-stricken youth from the ghettos of our great cities or even a son or a daughter from some rich mansion on the avenue. But let us not leave out of consideration the hitchhiker or the hippie trudging wearily along the nation's highways, hoping that some passing motorist will see his or her outstretched thumb. Maybe that is the promised prophet for whom the grace of God has been waiting.

And as Samuel McCaulay Lindsay, eloquent Baptist preacher now living in Florida at the age of ninety and more, said in my hearing at the New York State Baptist Convention some years ago, "The grace of God is that quality in the heart of God which leads him to treat us better than we deserve."

[3] Quoted from Edwin T. Dahlberg, *Herald of the Evangel* (St. Louis: Bethany Press, 1965), p. 192.
[4] *Ibid.*

9

Should We Legalize Hitchhiking?

Two roadside encounters—one with a hitchhiker and the other with a woman driver—illustrate the need for legislation protecting hitchhiker and driver alike.

One of the most unusual passengers to whom I have ever given a ride was a young Mexican I found standing beside the road outside the city of Las Vegas, New Mexico, just at dawn, as I was on my way to the Raton Pass and on to Denver, Colorado.

Probably no hitchhiker ever needed a ride more desperately than this teenager. He was carrying an armful of oil cans filled with motor oil, a rather awkward burden. While he was riding with one of his friends from Denver to Las Vegas the preceding night, their old car had run out of oil some twelve miles from Las Vegas. He had walked all the way to Las Vegas before he got to a gas station where he could buy some oil. Now he was walking back to the stalled car in which his friend was waiting. It was with a sense of obvious relief that he took the oil cans from his aching arms and placed them one by one on the floor of my car.

He could not speak English very well; so I had some difficulty in understanding the situation. I got the general idea, however, which was that we should soon be able to see the car that he said was standing on a ridge at the top of a slope some distance ahead.

We cruised slowly along on a four-lane highway that had an unusually wide median between the eastbound and westbound lanes. The early morning light just before dawn was still somewhat dim, so we had to keep a sharp lookout for the stalled car. It seemed as though we had gone more than twelve miles before we saw anything that looked like the car the young Mexican had described. Just as I was thinking that maybe we should turn around and cruise along the westbound lane to Las Vegas again in the effort to find the missing vehicle, the boy beside me suddenly exclaimed, "There it is!" He was right. The car was standing exactly where he said it would be, at the top of the ridge ahead of us. Thanking me profusely, my likable young Mexican friend picked up his precious oil cans and started for the opposite side of the highway. The last I saw of him, he was crossing the grassy median on his way to the waiting car where his partner had no doubt enjoyed a good night's sleep in the meantime. They were both looking for work, as so many hitchhikers are.

I had another unexpected experience more recently while driving home to Phoenix after an engagement in Tucson earlier in the day. As I was nearing Phoenix just before dusk, I saw a car ahead of me, parked on the shoulder of the highway and with its hood up as though in trouble. A young woman was sitting at the wheel. With every intention of playing the part of the good Samaritan, I slowed up behind her and got out of my car to inquire whether I could be of any help.

With great astonishment I saw the girl get out of her car, slam down the hood, and rush back into the car again. Taking off with a jackrabbit start, she went racing down the highway at top speed. By the time I got back into my own car again, she was already out of sight in the early twilight.

Who was she? What was her hurry? Whether in a last minute panic she thought I was propositioning her or intending to rob her I'll never know, but I admired her presence of mind. Four out of every five women whose bodies have been found in the Arizona desert in a year, either stabbed or beaten to death, have met their fate at the hands of rapists from whom they had accepted a ride. It is not without reason that the evening news reports on TV repeatedly emphasize police warnings to women and young girls against ever accepting rides from strangers.

It is important that in every state in the Union there should be legislation enacted which will protect the rights both of the drivers and the hitchhikers on our American highways. This protection is one reason why thoughtful attention should be paid to the efforts of the California hitchhiking lobby to get a measure through the legislature of that state with this end in view.

The California bill was introduced in 1972. It recommended the adoption of a system based upon the Polish model, in which the hitchhiker is checked for drug habits or criminal records and the driver receives contest coupons by which he or she is rewarded for giving the hitchhiker a lift. According to this plan the hitchhikers would pay a few dollars for entering the voluntary program. If the applicant is not a criminal or a fomer mental patient, he or she would be issued a coupon booklet. The coupons, indicating that the hitchhiker is "safe," would be given to drivers on the basis of how many miles they drove the hitchhiker. If the driver were lucky, he or she then would win a contest prize if the number was a winning one. This might encourage persons to help hitchhikers in need. The surplus money derived from the entrance fees would be used to finance the erection of youth hostels that would provide inexpensive overnight accommodations, a type of youth hospitality center that is already very popular in Europe.

Obvious difficulties would be involved in the implementing of the legislation just described. For one thing, there might easily be collusion between the driver and the rider as to their report on the number of miles the hitchhiker rode with the driver. Still further, forged certificates passed from one hitchhiker to another might pose another law enforcement problem. It would require an immense number of government inspectors to check on all these matters relating to evidences of fraud. Moreover, the "safe driver" and "safe hitchhiker" certificates would call for all manner of mental tests and vehicle inspections. Such an examination of driving records and criminal records could cause the whole system to bog down. The mass of paperwork alone could reach incredible proportions.

Another proposal in the California bill was to expand the State Highway Commission to eight members, one of whom would be a representative of the "hitchhiking public." The young lobbyists contended that hitchhiking should be recognized as a legitimate mode of travel that is as safe as other kinds of human activity.

I am inclined to agree with the views of the California hitchhiking lobby that their mode of travel is as legitimate as any other. We recognize the freedom of the seas, in spite of occasional piracy, the spate of oil spills, and pollution of the oceans. Should there not also be a doctrine of freedom of the highways—not only for pedestrians, but also for bicycle riders?

It is regrettable that when the first interstate highways were being built no provision was made for bicycle paths or for pedestrians. Probably the added cost of such roadways, however narrow the lanes, was prohibitive. It is encouraging to note, however, that cycle paths are being developed more and more, both along city streets and rural highways. When we think of the generous provision that has been made both for bicycle and pedestrian traffic in Denmark, the Netherlands, and other countries in Europe, it would seem reasonable to believe that equal consideration could be given to the cyclists and hitchhikers in the United States, particularly in view of the wide expanses of land available on this vast continent. What a pleasant sight it is within the narrow confines of Europe to see whole families, parents and children together, riding their bicycles on a Saturday or Sunday afternoon. Nothing could mean more to family life in America than encouragement of such a practice here. Moreover, it could be a contribution to the economy now that the fuel and energy crisis has become so acute. Bicycles are still among the cheapest and most enjoyable forms of transportation.

In the meantime, whether by legalizing hitchhiker traffic or by the personal initiative of people of goodwill, let us do everything in our power to help riders and drivers to become better acquainted with one another. There is too much suspicion and distrust all over America. We need to take to heart more than we do the biblical principle of human relations: "There is no fear in love . . . perfect love casts out fear" (1 John 4:18). That is the Christian concept. The more we practice that spirit of trust in one another, the greater will be the confidence established in every area of our national life. Such confidence is essential to the continuing progress of the nation; so badly has our confidence in every direction been shaken—in politics, economics, education, science and technology, even in religion and the home.

Here again a humble turning to God is imperative. We need to remember that the word "creed" and the word "credit" have a common Latin derivation. Both "creed" and "credit" go back to the Latin word *credere,* which means "to trust," "to believe," "to have faith." In the business world it means to have trust in someone's integrity in money matters and in the ability of that person to meet payments when due. In the religious world it is related to a confession of faith. As soon as we have no creed, no faith, no integrity, the whole structure of credit begins to collapse. There is a run on the bank. The confidence of man in his fellowman is fatally shaken.

This is the state of mind in which we find ourselves now. We hear it verbalized all around us every day, in such false generalizations as "politicians are nothing but a bunch of crooks"; "90 percent of the people on welfare wouldn't take a job it it was served up on a silver platter"; "the churches today are filled with nothing but a lot of hypocrites."

We must get out of this mood. With the help of God we can. If what I am trying to say in this book will contribute even in a small measure to the reader's faith in God and human beings—hitchhikers and drivers included—I shall be more than content with my experiences on America's Jericho Road.

10

Pilgrims of Peace

A young missionary to the Indians of Arizona had to begin his work on the reservation a year or two ago without the use of a car. Undaunted, he walked long distances while visiting his flock. As a result of his faithful ministry on foot he gained the admiration of the Indians, who gave to him the name "The White Man Who Walked."

Comparatively few people do much walking today, unless it be for exercise. The automobile has made us so accustomed to riding that we are often reluctant to walk even the few blocks from the house to the church or to the nearest store. As for myself, I must confess that I am in this respect a sinner also. I am very thankful, however, that in the days of my youth I had to walk long distances. The high school I attended in Minneapolis was two miles from our home; so the round trip added up to four miles daily. I had an afternoon paper route also. Delivering the papers to my 175 customers called for a six-mile walk around the entire circuit every day. So it added up to ten miles a day, not counting the extra distances covered while on neighborhood errands or visiting some of my friends. I still love to walk. Now at the age of eighty-five years, I get up every morning at 6 o'clock and take a mile walk before breakfast.

Nothing could be more enjoyable. What Jeremy Taylor, winner of scholarly fame at Cambridge University as a prolific writer, eloquent preacher, and chaplain to the king said early in the seventeenth century concerning the advantages of early rising is much to the point. "In the morning," he said, "when you awake, accustom yourself to think first upon God, or something in order to His service . . . and sometimes be curious to see the preparation which the sun makes, when he is coming forth from his chambers in the east." [1]

[1] From the book compiled by Frederick Ward Kates, *Moments with the Devotional Masters* (Nashville: The Upper Room, 1961), p. 43.

It is indeed a time to think upon God, to meditate, and to pray, as the sun comes up in all the glory and splendor of the dawn. Equally mysterious and beautiful is the departure of the moon at almost the same hour, as it takes its leave from the duties of the night. There is a certain period in the three-quarter phase of the moon when it resembles a great silver football high above the earth, sailing through the skies as if some celestial being had flung a mighty forward pass from midfield in space into the outstretched arms of a receiver waiting for it at some goal line beyond the horizon. Besides all this there are the trees standing tall and still with not a leaf stirring, the birds singing their morning song, the dogs barking in the distance, and the roosters crowing.

There might be those who would say that the average hitchhiker is insensitive to all these mysteries of nature around him. Not so! Recall, if you will, the young man mentioned in an earlier chapter of this book, who after sitting for two hours by the side of the road before being picked up, said to me when I asked him how long he had been waiting, "The time passed quickly. I have been thinking about God and the beauty of the world he has made." Others have spoken to me in the same terms.

While the majority of the hitchhikers requesting a ride might not be quite so aware of God's creation as was the youth just referred to, I have met a considerable number who have been very conscious of their *need* of God, especially in the world within their own souls. They respond with surprising celerity when questioned about the state of that world.

One such person was a twenty-year-old Catholic boy who stood waiting at the ramp leading up to one of our western freeways. He had left his home in the East just a few weeks earlier in the hopes of visiting his nineteen-year-old girl friend. They had been high school sweethearts from the time they met until they graduated. Since their graduation she had moved to the West, but they had corresponded faithfully with each other and seen each other from time to time. He felt great consternation when he himself came West to find that she was living with another man without benefit of marriage. So crushed was he by this discovery that he was in complete despair. I have rarely met a man so utterly brokenhearted.

Now he was hitchhiking his way back home to his parents. It was only eight o'clock in the morning when I first found him standing beside the ramp, waiting for a ride. He was a handsome lad, in spite of his patched jeans, somewhat disheveled hair, and one- or two-day-old growth of beard. I took an instant liking to him because of his courteous manner and seeming intelligence and character. He rode with me nearly all day. It was four o'clock in the afternoon by the time we got to Phoenix, from which point he was hoping to pick up another ride with someone going farther east.

Having been with me the entire day, he shared the whole story of his troubles along the way, especially at lunch time. I had invited him to be my guest at a small but very beautiful inn at Blythe, California, where I frequently get a bite to eat when going back and forth between Phoenix and Los Angeles. It was significant, I thought, that as he looked at the lovely little New England type structure we were about to enter, with its red brick walls, white window frames, green lawns, and gorgeous flower beds, he said with some embarrassment, "I don't think I look good enough to go into such a nice place as this."

"Sure you do!" I replied. "The customers here are everyday folks, just like us. All you need to do is wash up a bit in the rest room and comb your hair. Here—take my pocket comb."

He took the comb with gratitude and with a kind of natural grace. When he came back from the rest room, he looked clean and refreshed. His dark hair was neatly combed, and his shirt was tucked in. Altogether, his whole bearing gave evidence of a heightened self-respect.

Although I suggested a more hearty lunch, he seemed reluctant as my guest to give the waitress anything more than a modest order. Sensing his hesitation, I followed his example and had a very light lunch myself. As we finished eating, he said suddenly, "I think I am going to make a long-distance phone call to my folks to let them know I am on my way home."

When he came back to the table after the phone call, his face was shining. "I talked with my mother," he reported enthusiastically. "She was just great—mighty happy, too, when I told her I was coming home."

Sharing his joy, I suggested that we go back to the car where we could talk a little bit more freely. As we sat in the car, facing some of the most colorful flower beds I have ever seen, he opened his heart to me freely as I listened.

"My father and mother are wonderful," he said. "They go to the Catholic church—are pretty religious and all that stuff. I go to the Catholic church, too, but I'm afraid I'm not too good at it."

At that point he seemed to return to his mood of dejection as he brought up again the subject of his broken love affair.

"I just can't get over it. How could she do what she has done to me? I don't think I'll ever get any happiness out of life again. She meant everything to me. I thought our love was the real thing." After a few moments of silence, while he sat buried in his thoughts, I attempted as gently as possible to comfort and counsel him. I told him of friends of mine who in the days of their youth had also suffered broken engagements, who had been so utterly disillusioned as to lose all faith in God, to say nothing of losing all faith in the opposite sex. Usually when young people come into a pastor's study and say that they can't believe in God any more, they really are saying, "I can't believe in *her*"; or "I can't believe in *him*." Disillusionment with people often precedes a person's loss of faith in God. But it works both ways. Sometimes it is the rejection of faith in God which makes people cynical about human beings.

So I approached the young hitchhiker's needs from both directions. Referring again to the friends of mine who in the long ago had been jilted by their sweethearts even after the joy of what they had thought was a lasting love, I pointed out how many of these young men had, after their initial despair, met a fine girl, married her, and had a happily married life for the rest of their days. Urging him to recover his faith in womanhood and to believe confidently that a better experience of romance was still awaiting him in the future, I then began to call attention to the sources of a religious faith.

Drawing out the little New Testament that I always carry in my hip pocket and turning to the words of the apostle Paul in Acts 9:4-6, I said:

"Here is the story of a man who had lost everything. He had once had a respected position in his community, with a fine background of education that enabled him to reach a place of immense power and prestige as one of the top religious leaders of the nation. Then one day on the road to Damascus while on a mission designed to destroy the new religion that posed a threat to his own religious faith, he had a vision in which he met the risen Christ. Falling to the ground in terror, he heard a voice saying, 'Why are you persecuting me?' He cried out in amazement and said, 'Who are you, Lord?' The voice came again. 'I am Jesus, whom you are persecuting; but rise and enter into the city, and you will be told what you are to do.' When Paul rose to his feet, he found that he had been completely blinded by the vision. For three days he was without sight and had to depend on those who were with him to lead him by the hand into the city of Damascus.

"Giving up everything in his past life—fame, friends, a big reputation, and all the comforts of life—Paul became a follower of Jesus and finally was put into prison because he had joined up with the Christians. Now listen to what he wrote in a letter while still in prison and probably in chains: '. . . one thing I do, forgetting what lies behind and straining forward to what lies ahead, I press on toward the goal for the prize of the upward call of God in Christ Jesus' (Philippians 3:13-14).

"Paul's experience was of course very different from yours. So far as we know, he never married. But he had suffered a crushing loss of everything that most people would give their lives to possess. He wrote, 'I have suffered the loss of all things, and count them as refuse, in order that I may gain Christ' (Philippians 3:8). So don't you think it would be possible for you, too, to forget what lies behind you—all the unhappy experiences with your girl friend—and look to the future? Should you look maybe even to the call of God in Christ Jesus, as Paul did?"

This seemed to get to him. "Maybe you're right!" he exclaimed.

All the rest of the day he was in an optimistic mood. He wanted to know all about my faith as a Baptist as well as about my family and my work. We touched on many phases of religion and on life generally. Arriving in Phoenix at about 4 P.M., he said as he prepared to leave me in the hopes of catching a ride that would take him farther on his journey home, "Could you give me your name and address? I would like to write to you after I get back to my folks. Could I keep in touch with you?"

I told him that would please me very much. So I gave him my card and then pulled up at the side of the street for a farewell prayer. One of the last things he said as he was getting out of the car was, "Thank you especially for that Bible verse you gave me about forgetting what is behind and looking to the future. I'm going to try to remember that and to live up to it."

Since only a few days have elapsed since I said good-bye to him, I have not at this writing heard from him, but I am confident that I will, just as I have from others after many weeks and sometimes months have gone by. Most of the younger generation today are not very proficient in letter writing. They are more dependent on the telephone and on recordings. I earnestly hope that whether or not I ever hear from him, he may some day be able to say, "Not that I have already obtained this or am already perfect; but I press on to make it my own, because Christ Jesus has made me his own" (Philippians 3:12).

Many thoughts come to me as I see people walking, whether they are hitchhikers on the highways, old people walking with canes and crutches in homes for the aging, little toddlers taking their first steps and falling into the outstretched arms of their mothers or their fathers, lovers strolling hand in hand along an ocean shore, families walking to church together as they go down a shaded street in a small town, or the busy throngs hurrying along the sidewalks of a big city as they rush to their lunch appointments and back to the office again.

The Bible has much to say about the way we walk—not so much the particular place we walk nor the distance, but rather the mood and spirit in which we walk and the way of life we follow in our relationship to God and to others. Some of those who walked and are mentioned in the Bible, whether good or evil, are the following:

"Enoch walked with God" (Genesis 5:22).

"Amon was twenty-two years old when he began to reign, and. . . . he forsook the Lord, the God of his fathers, and did not walk in the way of the Lord" (2 Kings 21:19-22).

"Blessed is the man who walks not in the counsel of the wicked" (Psalm 1:1).

"Even though I walk through the valley of the shadow of death, I fear no evil" (Psalm 23:4).

"He that walketh in a perfect way" (Psalm 101:6, KJV).

"A poor man who walks in his integrity" (Proverbs 19:1).

"The people who walked in darkness have seen a great light" (Isaiah 9:2).

"For you have not walked in my statutes . . . but have acted according to the ordinances of the nations that are round about you" (Ezekiel 11:12).

"And to walk humbly with your God" (Micah 6:8).

"As he walked by the Sea of Galilee, he saw two brothers. . . . and he said to them 'Follow me, and I will make you fishers of men'" (Matthew 4:18-19).

"And they were on the road, going up to Jerusalem, and Jesus was walking ahead of them; and they were amazed, and those who followed were afraid. And taking the twelve again, he began to tell them what was to happen to him" (Mark 10:32).

"And he said to them, 'What is this conversation which you are holding with each other as you walk?' And they stood still, looking sad" (Luke 24:17).

"Look carefully then how you walk, not as unwise men but as wise, making the most of the time, because the days are evil" (Ephesians 5:15-16).

". . . walk by the Spirit, and do not gratify the desires of the flesh" (Galatians 5:16).

"And walk in love, as Christ loved us and gave himself up for us" (Ephesians 5:2).

These are only a few of the hundreds of Bible references to the manner of our walking.

Some of the familiar lines of Christian hymns and songs are a great help to our frame of mind when we walk. Typical among them are "I walked today where Jesus walked," "When we walk with the

Lord," "Trying to walk in the steps of the Saviour," and the words from Seth Parker's old song, "You go to your church and I'll go to mine, but let's walk along together." One that especially appeals to me when on a long walk through the country is the one with the repeated refrain, "I wonder as I wander, out under the sky." Singing as we walk can often lighten the burden of weary feet and heighten our appreciation of the beauties of nature that are everywhere around us.

Probably the most notable walker of our time is the remarkable woman who identifies herself only as the "Peace Pilgrim." It has been my good fortune to meet her many times through the years, to hear her speak, and to carry on a personal correspondence with her. No one that I know has given me more encouragement in working for world peace than she has. Not only that, but she is a shining example of that inner peace which comes from a right relationship with one's inner self and from constant communion with God as well as with his children everywhere.

Maybe the best way I can introduce her is with a quotation from the news services as they announce her coming and going, whether in Mexico, Alaska, Canada, or other areas of our vast continent:

> You may see her walking through your town or along the highway—a silver-haired woman dressed in navy blue slacks, and a short tunic with pockets all around the bottom in which she carries all her worldly possessions. It says "PEACE PILGRIM" in white letters on the front of the tunic and "25,000 MILES ON FOOT FOR PEACE" on the back. She has finished walking those miles, but she continues to walk, for her vow is: "I shall remain a wanderer until mankind has learned the way of peace, walking until I am given shelter and fasting until I am given food." She walks without a penny in her pockets and she is not affiliated with any organization. She walks as a prayer and as a chance to inspire others to pray and work with her for peace. She speaks to individuals along the way, to groups in cities, through the medium of the news services. She points out that this is a crisis period in human history, and that we who live in the world today must choose between a nuclear war of annihilation and a golden age of peace.[2]

She defines her magic formula for peace as follows: (1) "There is a magic formula for resolving conflicts. It is this: Have as your objective the resolving of the conflict—not the gaining of advantage." (2) "There is a magic formula for avoiding conflicts. It is this: Be concerned that you do not offend—not that you are not offended."

Among the hundreds of tributes that have come to her from people in all walks of life, I believe one of the finest and most revealing was from a man who picked her up and gave her a ride one

[2] Reprinted from literature written and published by the Peace Pilgrim herself.

day as she was walking along the highway. He said in a letter he wrote to her: "What have you done to me? All I did was ask a nice lady if she wanted a ride, and I end up with a whole new world of wonders before me! Every day now my life is rapidly changing. I simply am not the man I was a month ago, a week ago—yesterday. I continue to find new meaning in our conversation."

As I read this man's testimony, I envied him. As I have said before concerning my experiences with hitchhikers, I don't make it a practice to pick up women. In any case, the Peace Pilgrim is not a hitchhiker. She rides only when invited to do so. But it would be a privilege to have a passenger as inspiring as she would be. Who knows? This might still be my good fortune, for in a recent letter she said:

I am delighted to receive your letter, and to learn that you are writing a book about your experiences with hitchhikers. Perhaps some day you will see me at the entrance to a freeway with my thumb out. Since I finished counting 25,000 miles of walking—toward the end of 1964—I have been walking intermittently and hitchhiking part of the way. . . . While counting miles I put walking first, then speaking, then answering mail—now I put speaking first, then answering mail, then walking. Within a year I'll have completed my sixth peace pilgrimage route—a five-year route. Next year in March (1978) I'll be heading for California to start a seventh peace pilgrimage route—a six-year route.

Her seventh peace pilgrimage route will take her through the forty-eight states in six years. Beginning with California, Oregon, Washington, and Nevada in 1978, she will continue her journey through all sections of the country year by year, concluding her trip by going along the Atlantic Coast from Maine to Florida.

People sometimes marvel at the distances I have traveled while picking up hitchhikers the past eight years—an average of eight to ten thousand miles every summer, from coast to coast. My experiences in this connection have been exciting and rewarding, but they are as nothing compared with the adventures the Peace Pilgrim has had. Let me quote just one story in her own words.

A True Story

It happened in the middle of the night in the middle of the desert. The traffic had just about stopped, and there wasn't a human habitation within many miles. I saw a car parked at the side of the road. The driver called to me saying, "Come on, get in and get warm." I said, "I don't ride." He said, "I'm not going anywhere, I'm just parked here." I got in. I looked at the man. He was a big, burly man—what most people could call a rough-looking individual. After we had talked awhile he said, "Say, wouldn't you like to get a few winks of sleep?" and I said, "Oh, yes, I certainly would!" and I curled up and went to sleep. When I awoke, I could see that the man was very puzzled about something, and after we had talked for quite some time, he admitted that when he had asked me to get into the car he had certainly meant me no good, adding, "When you curled up so trustingly and went to sleep, I just couldn't touch you." No one walks so safely as he who walks humbly and harmlessly, but with great love and great faith. For he gets through to the good in people—and there is good within everyone—and they cannot harm him. This works between individuals, it works between groups, and it would work between nations if nations had the courage to try it.[3]

This admittedly could have led into a dangerous situation. It might well be that only a woman as trusting and good as the Peace Pilgrim could have survived it. But when she says that no one walks as safely as those who walk humbly and harmlessly, I thoroughly agree. Her statement in this respect confirms what Raymond Wilson said regarding his practice of picking up hitchhikers, quoted in an earlier chapter of this book, "My experience has been that on the whole, I think it is better and safer to trust people than to fear them."[4] There is good biblical backing for this position. It was Job, cursing the day of his birth, who said "For the thing that I fear comes upon me, and what I dread befalls me" (Job 3:25).

Fear is always an invitation to disaster. As my older brother said to me one time, "If you enter a horse's stall, afraid that he will kick you, he always will." If, on the other hand, you enter in quiet confidence, speaking to him gently and soothingly, the chances are very good that the horse will respond with the same calm and trusting spirit. The horse that my brother was talking about was a mean one, always kicking the sides of the stall at the slightest provocation and even biting his mate without a cause when the lumber wagon they were pulling struck a stone in the road. Our theory was that he must have suffered from some kind of equine stomach ulcers! But my brother Arnold could always enter Pluto's stall in safety and without fear.

The critically dangerous and frightening times in which we live call for more people who will enter areas of contemporary conflict without fear. We must become "Pilgrims of Peace," not in some naive, sentimental way but in full awareness of the dangers. We must deliberately enter the danger zones in the hope of easing the tensions that threaten to destroy us.

While I have never been a hitchhiker on the highways of America, I have in some small measure been a walker for world peace and justice. This has been chiefly in connection with the many peace

[3] *Ibid.*
[4] E. Raymond Wilson, *Thus Far on My Journey* (Richmond, Ind.: Friends United Press, 1976), p. 20.

marches that characterized the 1960s and early 1970s, particularly the war years in Vietnam.

As a member of the Inter-Faith Peace Mission to Vietnam, sponsored by the Fellowship of Reconciliation in the midsummer season of 1965, I had an opportunity to see what the war was doing to that unhappy country even in the earliest stages of the conflict. It was at the time when the presence of our American troops in Vietnam were still supposed to be mainly in an "advisory" capacity.

I had been a member of the Fellowship of Reconciliation since 1916, so I was glad to accept the invitation to be one of the fifteen members of the Inter-Faith Peace Mission. They were from three major religious faiths: Jewish, Catholic, and Protestant.

In addition to the American members of the mission, we were joined in Saigon by two international associates. One of these was the famed Pastor Martin Niemoeller of Germany, member of the Presidium of the World Council of Churches and for seven years a prisoner of the Nazis because of his resistance to Adolf Hitler's liquidation of the Jews. The other was Pasteur André Trocmé, St. Gervais Reformed Church, Geneva, Switzerland, beloved pacifist and refugee relief worker of all Europe.

Previous to our departure for Vietnam, six of us had an hour and a half interview with United States Defense Secretary Robert McNamara, in which we presented the following five points of chief concern:

1. A cease-fire in Vietnam
2. Renewed efforts at a peaceful settlement
3. A stepped up program of economic development in the lower Mekong Valley
4. A definition of American objectives in Vietnam
5. Greater recourse to the United Nations, and less dependence on unilateral or bilateral action.

Mr. McNamara received us very courteously and discussed very frankly the points listed, indicating that there were factors both of agreement and disagreement; but he left us with the impression that his only answer was a military showdown. This impression was greatly heightened by the military setting of his office—artillery field pieces pointing at us—and especially by the ghastly charts showing the body count of the dead for every twenty-four hours of the week.

The military showdown lasted for many years. The final answer of the vast majority of the American people as of now—1977—seems to be, "We should never have been in Vietnam in the first place."

After several days in Vietnam, interviewing war correspondents,

United States Information officers, labor leaders, youth groups, International Volunteer Service workers, army officers, organizers of the Black Peace Corps, the patriarch of the Buddhist Institute, village officials, and as many others as possible, our team divided up into four sections. One group stayed in Saigon for further contacts; another went down to the Mekong Delta; another to Phnom Penh in Cambodia; and four of us went up to a combat area at Song Be, some seventy miles north of Saigon.

While on the flight to Song Be in an eight-passenger Beechcraft plane, we flew low over the rice fields of South Vietnam and then over the thick jungle territory farther north. This gave us an opportunity to see firsthand some of the ravages of war—the burned-out rice fields, the blasted rubber plantations standing out like so many white ghost trees, and the blackened ruins of deserted villages.

Song Be was the capital of the province and just two months before our arrival had been the scene of one of the bloodiest mass battles of the war. Three regiments of the Vietcong—about 2,500 men—attacked in force at 11:20 P.M. on May 11. According to Colonel Ma Sanh, the provincial chief, who was an old guerrilla fighter, and Major Mitchell Sakey, the American advisor, the Vietcong suicide squads tried in vain to climb over the high barbed-wire fences surrounding the administration building of the capital. The fighting continued furiously for hours until finally the Vietcong were repulsed. Major Sakey said it was difficult to determine the Vietcong losses, many having been buried in mass graves and others dying in the jungles after being mortally wounded. Some estimates placed the enemy losses as high as 765 killed, while of the 600 American and South Vietnamese defenders, only 5 lost their lives. The accuracy of these figures, however, may be doubtful.

It was dramatically evident during the day we were at Song Be that we were on the frontier of the active war zone. Only 150 yards away from the administration building in which we were being briefed, mortars were lobbing shells over into the jungle just beyond the airport at which we had landed only an hour earlier. At the same time we could hear the sound of an air strike only six or seven miles away. This was mostly for harassment, warning the Vietcong that their movements were being watched.

A sadder aspect of the day was seen a bit later. While we were having lunch in the mess hall, we were waited upon by a number of young Vietnamese women, apparently in their early twenties. All of them were already war widows, according to Major Sakey. The military gave widows jobs so they could support their children.

Following the luncheon we saw another tragic by-product of the war. Preceded by an armed escort in a jeep to guard against an ambush while on the way to the airport, we stopped at a refugee camp where several hundred refugees were being housed. Most of them were old people or children. The children came swarming across the compound when they saw us, shouting "Okay!" in the hopes of getting some bubble gum. Some of the mothers and grandparents followed them. One of the American soldiers who had come with us—a big, genial top sergeant from North Carolina—suddenly gave an exclamation of distress as he discovered that except for a few leftover pieces from the last trip, he had no more bubble gum. The children were likewise very disappointed.

I have always had a great admiration for the soldier. This was true of Jesus also. Some of his highest praise was for the Roman army captains and for their men. It was a Roman centurion, also, who when standing on guard at the foot of the cross said as he watched the dying Savior, "Truly this man was a son of God!" (Mark 15:39).

I could not help admiring the sergeant from North Carolina. Obviously he loved children and was genuinely concerned when he found he was without his usual supply of bubble gum. And yet I could not escape the irony of a situation in which he was required to destroy life when under orders, at the same time that he gave out bubble gum to the children of friend and foe when obeying the promptings of his heart. This seemed to me to be the policy of the war in Vietnam—a bubble gum policy by which we practically destroyed a nation in the effort to save it.

Whether or not our mission contributed anything to the final ending of the war, none of us can say. We had frequent opportunities for press interviews as well as for public addresses at a number of meetings and open forums, including a debate with Senator Goldwater before a thousand young high school people from all over Arizona. All this may have helped enlighten people as to what was going on in Southeast Asia and create a measure of public opinion in favor of bringing the war to an end by negotiation. We could not see many other visible results. We cabled from Hong Kong a message to President Johnson in which we expressed the unanimous findings of our entire team: An early termination of the war by a negotiated peace was imperative. However, we received no answer from him. When we interviewed the Secretary of State and the Secretary of Labor following our return, they were all firm in their opinion that a military victory was the only answer. As we know now, no such victory ever came. The experience in Vietnam, Laos, and Cambodia was one of the sorriest chapters in the history of this nation and one of the saddest in the history of Vietnam as well.

This is one of the reasons why I have participated in so many peace marches all over the United States—in Seattle, San Francisco, New York, Philadelphia, Phoenix, and Washington, D.C. Like the Peace Pilgrim, I have felt an inner compulsion to walk for peace, or even to stand still for peace, both here in my home city of Phoenix, Arizona, and in Washington, D.C. Standing still for peace is simply a way of describing the prayer vigils in which we stood still before God on the grounds of the national capital or on the downtown sidewalks and curbstones of various communities throughout the country. In many ways the prayer vigils invited more scorn and abuse than the peace marches did. One of the most unpleasant experiences I have had anywhere was on one evening in Phoenix when a small group of some thirty people stood in a thin line at the street side of the Park Central parking lot. This is one of the busiest shopping centers in the downtown area of the city. A man parked in a car just behind me, opposite the sidewalk, got out of his car and for nearly ten minutes carried on a tirade of profanity and obscene language directed at me such as I have never had hurled at me in my entire life. Receiving no reply, he finally ceased, got into his car, stepped on the throttle, backed out of his parking space, and roared angrily away.

Probably the most dramatic peace march of them all was the "March Against Death" in Washington, D.C., when many thousands of demonstrators marched from 6 P.M. on Thursday evening until 10 A.M. on Saturday morning. Our Arizona delegation was the second in the line of march, just behind the delegation from Alabama. Beginning at Arlington Cemetery in Virginia and crossing the bridge across the Potomac, we marched four abreast down Pennsylvania Avenue, past the White House, and on to the Capitol building, where each delegation disbanded. The various sections of the procession marched only five hours—in our case as Arizonans from 6 to 11 P.M. But the last of the demonstrators did not arrive at the finish line at the back of the Capitol building until ten o'clock Saturday forenoon, so many were the marching thousands. It was a peaceful and most solemn demonstration. Each of us wore a cardboard placard with the name of a soldier lost in Vietnam. I carried the name of the son of one of our American Baptist pastors and his wife, the Reverend and Mrs. Rudolph Loidolt of Phoenix, Arizona. This fine young man had been sent into the battle line in Southeast Asia within a few weeks of his arrival overseas, was badly wounded, and died after a long period of surgery and suffering.

As we passed the White House, each one of us turned and faced President Nixon's window, stood silent for a moment, called out the name of the war victim whose name we bore, and then resumed the march until reaching a point at the rear of the Capitol building. Placed there were several coffins into which we deposited the names of the dead as two drummers sounded the solemn "Long Roll" on their drums.

It was an experience of profound emotion for us all. Leading the march were a father and mother with their son, a veteran of the war in Vietnam whose brother had been killed in action. Along the line of march, in addition to the traffic police, were parade marshals appointed by the organizers of the demonstration to maintain order. As we came to each traffic corner, they stopped us when the red light went on, in order that the bumper to bumper line of cars might go through without delay. It was simply one evidence of our concern that there might be full compliance with every requirement of the law so that the public might in no way be inconvenienced. There could not have been a more eloquent example of the American right of democratic protest at the highest level.

In spite of all the unfavorable publicity so often encountered by those who have taken a firm stand for peace even in wartime, there are indications now that the message is at last getting through to the rank and file of the people. If I were presented with an opportunity now, I would at the age of eighty-five continue to walk, whether for international peace, racial peace, or any other kind of just and righteous peace; for I believe this is in keeping with the spirit of him whom we call the Prince of Peace.

I believe, too, that this is the way of the future. One of the great satisfactions I have had in marching side by side with the pilgrims of peace in so many areas of the country has been my joy as an octogenarian to find myself marching side by side with the *young*. It is the young who must carry the banner into the future. For as the late L.P. Jacks said in his exhilarating book, *The Confession of an Octogenarian,* an octogenarian is by definition "a trespasser in the universe," who should have the decency to keep silence and "not aggravate the trespass by inflicting his confession on the hearing of lawful wayfarers who, though still within the Psalmist's boundaries of three score years and ten, have enough labor and sorrow of their own."[5]

The young are under no necessity to keep silence. They can speak

[5] Lawrence Pearsall Jacks, *Confession of an Octogenarian* (New York: The Macmillan Company, 1942), p. 249.

and must speak if our civilization is to survive the fever of hate and enmity now raging around the circles of the globe. Not only must they speak up for peace but also for the kind of world organization that will have the authority to enforce the peace. The United Nations is one step in that direction. As an open forum where nations may enter into dialogue and thus begin to clarify the issues, it has already proved to be of immense value. But it lacks power. What needs to be done now is to develop a form of world federalism something along the line of Norman Cousins's plea for a world sovereignty, a world court, and a world police force that will have the power to enforce the necessary international law. This will involve some degree of willingness on the part of the individual nations to surrender some measure of their national sovereignty. This is the critical issue.

As it is now, every country is a law unto itself, just as was the case with the individual states of our own nation before the federal constitution was adopted. If the colonies had not merged their sovereignties in the overall sovereignty of the United States of America, where would we be today? Our founding fathers were smart enough to foresee that; so they created a federal union with a nationwide authority that nevertheless protected the rights of the separate states. Why cannot we be smart enough to see the necessity for an international sovereignty today? The matter is so urgent; immense issues are at stake, issues that cannot be settled by the affected nations separately. What are to be the fishing limits in coastal waters? What agency shall control the traffic in outer space? Who is to determine the rights of ownership of the limitless agricultural resources and of the oil and mineral deposits of the sea?

We need to remember the view of our world as seen by one of the astronauts returning from the moon, who described the earth as a lovely globe of mystical blue, without any of the national borders that we see on the maps that humankind has made. It was only after humankind created national borders that the troubles began.

We must return to the vision so well expressed by our Lord Jesus Christ in the Lord's Prayer: "Thy kingdom come, thy will be done, on earth as it is in heaven." His world was one world. And God loved that world. He loved it so much that Jesus could say of Him, "God sent the Son into the world, not to condemn the world, but that the world might be saved through him" (John 3:17).

One of the best ways we can hallow the name of God is to become pilgrims of peace, striving to fulfil the biblical prophecy recorded almost word for word both in Isaiah 2:4 and in Micah 4:3. Which one of these two prophets was quoting the other or whether both of them were quoting an earlier and unknown writer cannot be known for certain. But they were in agreement when writing some of the most sublime words ever penned by man. Describing what will happen when God shall sit in final judgment upon the nations and decide for many peoples, both Isaiah and Micah are reported as saying, "They shall beat their swords into plowshares, and their spears into pruning hooks; nation shall not lift up sword against nation, neither shall they learn war any more."

In other words, all military training will come to an end. It may well be that God is already deciding among the nations and that his judgments have already gone forth. What more terrible warnings could possibly come to us than those we have experienced already in the destructive wars of our own century and in the development of nuclear bombs that have in them the potential to wipe out the last vestige of human life from the planet earth?

Truly has G. G. D. Kilpatrick said in his exposition of Isaiah 2:4:

> We have in each generation the strange, tragic spectacle of men endowed with genius, yet wholly unable to learn the art of living together in peace. Even with bitter experience of the horrors of war, every proposal for peace is basically related to the use of brute force. It is a question to ponder, how long the patience of Almighty God will be shown to a people bent on self-annihilation. It may well be that we are rapidly coming to the place in history where a last chance is offered to humanity to consider the terms God has laid down for life on this earth; to consider, to accept and obey, or to perish miserably.
>
> For such a moment the prophecy of Isaiah about world peace has a supreme and crucial relevance. . . . No serious mind can dismiss such a vision as unrelated to life. At every point it touches the contemporary situation.[6]

Having, as L. P. Jacks would say, "ventilated my notions" on everything from hitchhiking to war and peace and many things in between, I will now conclude the case for picking up hitchhikers, so many of whom I have found to be opposed to war—enough so to be potential pilgrims of peace if they can be persuaded to walk in the way of Him who said, "I am the way, and the truth, and the life" (John 14:6).

Fortunately there are many followers of the non-Christian religions who are also pilgrims of peace. Among the greatest of these was surely the Hindu, Mahatma Gandhi. I shall never forget the posters I saw all over India, especially in the schools and post offices, on my first visit to India in 1952–1953. The posters showed the picture

---

[6] G. G. D. Kilpatrick, in *The Interpreter's Bible,* ed. George A. Buttrick, 12 vols. (Nashville: Abingdon Press, 1956), vol. 5, pp. 180-181.

of a long and lonely road winding toward a far horizon. On it was a solitary figure walking with staff in hand but shown only from the waist down. At the bottom were the words "HE SHOWED US THE WAY." Everybody in India knew instinctively that it was the figure of Mahatma Gandhi, who, in spite of the fact that he was not a confessing Christian, walked down the same lonesome road that Jesus walked.

I know of no better way of summing up what I have tried to say in the chapters of this book than by quoting the words with which the Peace Pilgrim concluded a letter which she wrote to me in April, 1977:

> I journey easily and joyously. I walk because God gives me strength to walk. I live because God gives me supply to live. I speak because God gives me words to speak. Part of a religious life is a loving attitude toward people and an obedient attitude toward God. If you obey God, you grow to live in the constant awareness of God's presence—and fear is gone. If you love people, you reach the good in them—which is always there, no matter how deeply it may be buried. I know that all good effort bears good fruit—and it matters not whether the fruit becomes manifest in my life time.

My prayer as I have now passed my eighty-fifth birthday is that to the very end of my days on earth I may be able to say with Job, "I searched out the cause of him I did not know." At least I know the hopes and dreams of the hitchhikers on America's Jericho Road better now than when I picked up that first old saddle bum in Wyoming nearly ten years ago.

May God walk by the side of all these American nomads, old and young, as they travel the highways of the nation. And if they are never quite sure of the direction they should go when the sun rises in the morning, may they take to heart the words of him who said to Thomas the night before shouldering the heavy Roman cross:

> "I am the way, and the truth and the life; no one comes to the Father, but by me" (John 14:6).

11

Longing for the Eternal

We all want something to long for—something to believe in. This is basically what the hitchhikers on America's Jericho Road are seeking also. My conversations with them have convinced me that once you have established rapport with them, they reach out eagerly for a faith by which to live. Some of them may be shiftless vagabonds, but many of them have gone through tragic crises—failure in school; a broken love affair; a spirit of total misunderstanding between themselves and their parents; continuing inability to find a job; and, in some cases, an overwhelming temptation to which they have yielded, leaving them with a heavy burden of guilt and loss of all faith in God.

Something to long for and something to believe in? Even that is not enough. The truly Christian answer is found not in something to believe in, but *Someone* to believe in. I would go still further. The cry of the human heart finally is for Someone who *longs for us* and *believes in us.* This is the point of America's deepest need, not only in the life of the hitchhiker but also in the life of the entire nation. Only as we become acutely aware of this and cry out for the grace of God to enter into the personal lives of us all, can there by any hope of a change of direction in the moral and spiritual life of the nation.

The time has come for every follower of Christ to take a bold stance in his or her Christian witness—not only for the sake of some group such as the hitchhikers, but also for the sake of our entire culture. The prophet Isaiah, in the days of the Old Testament, said it well. Addressing the men and women in the sixth century B.C., he summoned them to a "high altitude" religion. The bitter years of the exile in Babylon were drawing to a close. The mind of the nation was still so overshadowed by the suffering and sorrow of those years that the people were in a mood of utter cynicism and despair. It was during that period of hopelessness concerning the national future that the prophet challenged the people to remember that God still occupied the center of the stage. In one of the loftiest passages to be found anywhere in the Scriptures, he cried out to them as follows:

> Get you up to a high mountain,
> O Zion, herald of good tidings;
> lift up your voice with strength,
> O Jerusalem, herald of good tidings,
> lift it up, fear not;
> say to the cities of Judah,
> "Behold your God!"
>
> Isaiah 40:9

We are living in a time of unprecedented bewilderment and uncertainty as to what the future holds. The call of Isaiah for a high altitude religion still comes down to us across the centuries as one of the most relevant messages to our own generation: to get up to a high mountain, to banish our fears, and to lift up our voices with strength as we herald the good tidings, "Behold your God!"

Many people are growing weary of endless "studies in depth." This phrase has become a cliché. All too often it is only a cover for shallow thinking, for inexcusable delay, and for surveys that are little more than evasion of desperately needed action.

All honor to faithful scientists, psychiatrists, and research people who have made truly profound studies in depth, revealing hidden areas of human experience and motivation that we needed to know. But let us now leave it to the scuba divers, the frogmen, and spelunkers of our frustrations to grope about in the murky depths of gloom and disillusionment while the community of faith follows the lead of such immortals as Isaiah, Martin Luther King, Jr., and others in the climbing of the mountain, to report to an astonished and unbelieving world, "We have climbed the mountain. And we have seen the kingdom of our God!"

Bishop Henry Knox Sherrill of the Episcopal Church, who was the first president of the National Council of Churches of Christ in the U.S.A., voiced the feelings of many of us at an all-day meeting of subsequent presidents of the Council, held in Boston a few years ago. During the morning session we had been discussing some of the most vital national and international issues of the time: war and peace, campus unrest, racial integration, economic injustice, family tensions, and the future of the ecumenical movement. Following the luncheon period, however, Bishop Sherrill spoke to us in an unusually thoughtful vein, and in quite another direction.

"Ladies and gentlemen," he said, "the subjects we were dealing with this morning are all of extreme importance, and of greatest concern to the future of our humanity. Throughout my ministry I have been an active participant in the movements endeavoring to find a solution to these problems. But I believe the time has come when we must go deeper. I am convinced that deep in the heart of the average man and woman today there is a great hunger for the Eternal. And unless the church of Jesus Christ can satisfy that hunger we shall have failed in our mission."

Rightly said! Bishop Sherrill's statement sobered us all. And it should sober not only the Christian churches and their constituencies, but also the whole American public. Unless we turn from our preoccupation with the methods and techniques of our human relations to a greater dependence upon the grace of God, we shall find ourselves in a dead end. People all the way from the mansions on the avenues to the teeming tenements in the ghettos of the inner cities are like the multitudes Jesus looked upon with compassion because they were as sheep without a shepherd. People are hungry for bread—but also for something more than bread. They are tired, worried, and disillusioned. Important as the methods and techniques of human progress may be, to urge upon a weary public only more reforms, more legislation, and more patriotism is like whipping a horse that is already exhausted. Better now to think in terms of the famous motto of William Carey, pioneer missionary to India, when in his appeal to the churches of England he cried, "Attempt great things for God, expect great things from God."[1]

A revival of energy in the moral and spiritual life of the nation depends upon a revival of energy and hope in the life of the churches. This in turn depends upon a revival of energy and hope in the lives of individual Christians. We can receive the needed spiritual power only by returning to its source. That source is in God alone, as revealed in Jesus Christ. A mere intellectual assent to God, however, or a sentimental belief in God will not be enough for the current crisis of the spirit. There must be contrition, repentance, and commitment—a personal confession of Christ as Savior and Lord. It makes all the difference in the world what kind of a God we believe in: a vague, indifferent deity far removed from life, or the God and Father of Jesus Christ—a God of justice, righteousness, and truth, who rules the nations and at the same time loves us and wants us as individuals.

It would help us to understand more vividly the nature of God's

[1] From the book by William Carey, *An Enquiry into the Obligations to Use Means for the Conversion of Heathen* (London: Hodder and Stoughton, 1891).

love for us if we could think of Him in terms of an incident related recently by Dr. Donald G. Shockley, chaplain of Redlands University, Redlands, California. Speaking at the Church of the Beatitudes, Phoenix, Arizona, where a young man was being ordained into the ministry, Dr. Shockley delivered the charge to the candidate. Emphasizing the importance of a minister's faithfulness as a pastor, particularly in visiting the homes of his or her parishioners, Dr. Shockley referred to an experience of his own.

"A few weeks ago," he said, "we were having a little family gathering at our house one afternoon, when I began to feel very miserable, as though I were coming down with the flu. Finally I asked to be excused and suggested that no one come upstairs to do anything for me, since all I needed was to lie down, pull the covers over me, and go to sleep for a couple of hours."

He went on to tell us how just when he was about to fall asleep, he heard little footsteps coming slowly up the stairs. Soon he sensed that they were just outside the bedroom door. Then he heard the doorknob turning gently. As the door opened, he saw his little daughter coming in. Hesitatingly she asked, "Can I come in and hurt with you, Daddy?"

We live in a hurting world, full of wounded hearts and pain. It was into this kind of world that God came, in the person of Jesus Christ—not only to hurt with us, but also to heal us.

It is for us to take this message to heart and to live it. God expects his human servants to help carry out his will. No one can number the people who are crying out for someone to come and to help them.

I remember a morning in a St. Louis hospital when I was visiting a patient in the psychiatric ward who had recovered and was about to go home. As I was in prayer with him, thanking God for the evidence of his healing power, I was vaguely conscious of a strange cry up at the far end of the corridor. The fine layman whom I was visiting said to me as I was about to leave, "Pastor, would you stop in that boy's room and find out what's troubling him? He is a sixteen-year-old high school student who was brought in early today, so they tell me. He's been calling out like that ever since he came."

As I was walking up the corridor to the young lad's room, I could make out just one word, repeated over and over again in the most agonizing tones, "SOMEBODY! . . . SOMEBODY! . . ."

Ordinarily I would not visit a patient in the psychiatric ward without first discussing the situation with the psychiatrist. But as I paused just for a moment outside the door, the boy saw me and said questioningly, "Doctor? Sir?"

I stepped inside the room. "I'm not a doctor; I'm a minister," I said.

He repeated his question. "Doctor? Sir?" And then he added piteously, "Am I sunk? Am I done for?"

"No," I said gently. "You're not done for. God loves you, and you are going to get well."

Following a quiet prayer in which I invoked God's peace and comfort to surround him night and day, I took my leave. What the outcome of his condition was, I do not know, as it was my last day in St. Louis before leaving for a three-year assignment in Pennsylvania. But at least for the remaining time I was in the hospital that morning, he was quiet, and I heard his call no more.

Sometimes I wake up in the night and still hear that same call, coming in the middle of the night from a dark house somewhere in the world: from the foreign students in our American colleges, lonely and homesick in a strange land; from children whose fathers and mothers are about to separate; from men on death row in the penal institutions of America; from the unemployed in our great cities; from many of our world leaders, whether in the halls of Congress, the White House, or in the United Nations. From people in every condition, whether of high or of low degree, there come the echoes from around the globe—"SOMEBODY!"

Is there any one of us who has not at some time felt like joining in that cry for help? "Out of the depths have I cried unto thee, O Lord," said the psalmist (Psalm 130:1, KJV). There is no one so self-sufficient that he or she does not turn to someone outside himself or herself for deliverance. Fortunate is that person who finds a human friend responding. Fortunately for all of us, there is a Divine Friend ready at all times to respond. "Seek the Lord while he may be found, call upon him while he is near; let the wicked forsake his way, and the unrighteous man his thoughts; let him return to the Lord, that he may have mercy on him, and to our God, for he will abundantly pardon" (Isaiah 55:6-7). The prophet makes clear that there are certain conditions which we must follow: penitence, commitment, faith, and a righteous life. "Then you shall call, and the Lord will answer; you shall cry, and he will say, Here I am" (Isaiah 58:9). Indeed, Isaiah went so far as to say to the people that if they complied with the moral and spiritual conditions of the divine will, they would hear God saying to them, "Before they call I will answer, while they are yet speaking I will hear."

These promises of the Old Testament were powerfully confirmed and enhanced by the coming of Jesus Christ into the world. "God shows his love for us in that while we were yet sinners Christ died for us" (Romans 5:8). This is the joyous assurance of our Christian faith. As Jesus himself said to the twelve the night before he went to the cross, "You did not choose me, but I chose you and appointed you that you should go and bear fruit and that your fruit should abide; so that whatever you ask the Father in my name, he may give it to you. This I command you, to love one another" (John 15:16-17).

There are those who would ridicule the idea of there being such a God, or even a God of any kind. An acquaintance of mine who is widely read and of great intelligence denies completely the existence of any of the religious values that for many of us constitute the very heart of our faith. He does not believe in God, he does not believe in life after death, he does not believe he has a soul. This philosophy of materialism leaves us with hardly any other alternative but the life of a zombie—the superstition which persuades certain followers of the voodoo religions of the West Indies to believe that a corpse may be brought to a trancelike state of animation by malevolent beings. Yet the friend I have mentioned is a good man. What may be the hidden experiences deep in the soul like roadblocks barring the way to the joy of the Christian life only God can know. Argumentation is of little help. Only a sincere witness to one's own experience of God's love is of any avail.

It is interesting that in a recent conversation with the man just described, he raised the question, "What is the meaning of the phrase we so often read about since Jimmy Carter was elected president, that people must be 'born again?'"

I read to him from the third chapter of John the story of Jesus' interview with Nicodemus, one of the religious leaders of Jerusalem, who came to Jesus one night and asked him about the way to the kingdom of God. It was in answering this question that Jesus said, "Unless one is born anew, he cannot see the kingdom of God." By this, Jesus meant that it was necessary to start all over again, to adopt new ways of thinking and action—in short, to begin a new life that would be pleasing to God. It was in this connection that Jesus called the attention of Nicodemus and of all the world since that time to the eagerness of the heavenly Father that every human being should have eternal life and that the whole world should be saved from its sin and despair (John 3:16-17).

It seems so difficult for countless numbers of people to understand this truth concerning the necessity of a new birth; it is still more difficult for them to accept it and act upon it. How happy is the person who does accept it and act upon it! And how blessed are those nations that take even the first steps in that direction.

No one needs this message more than the hitchhiker on our American highways. Restless, troubled, and often resented by his or her family and by the public at large, the hitchhiker is never forgotten by the eternal God. God cares. As Dr. John Bailey, of Edinburgh University, said in a great sermon at an ecumenical Lenten service of the Metropolitan Church Federation of Greater St. Louis: "My job is to teach history. That is what I am paid for." Holding up his Bible so all of us could see, he then said, "But when I read this book, I find an entirely different kind of history from that which the world understands as history. For on every page of this book I find the message that God wants us and loves us."

This is the message that the hitchhiker needs, as do all the rest of us: Not only does God care, but also there are people who care. A young minister expressed it eloquently when, in a letter I received from him during a time of great trial which tested his faith to the uttermost, he said regarding a number of his fellow alumni who had graduated from the same seminary he did and who stood by him in a brave stand he had taken, "I guess those guys are a pretty caring bunch!"

There may be those who would say, "Well, sure, we ought to care about people who are deserving citizens, like that young preacher. But hippies? Most of them are a headache to their own families and a nuisance to communities all over America. Why should we go out of our way to help them? Let them shift for themselves. Then maybe they won't be so shiftless."

This kind of attitude so prevalent in the older generation is out of keeping with the mind of Christ. Nor does it measure up to the spirit of Job in the Old Testament, "I searched out the cause of him whom I did not know" (Job 29:16).

It may well be that the nondescript young hitchhiker trudging wearily along the highway may represent more potential for the future of America than we now realize. He may not look like a very important person to the automobile driver who is hurrying to an appointment in the next town. But who knows? God may have great and important things in store for that person.

Probably no one who saw a young man backpacking his way through the wilderness of Wisconsin and Michigan into Canada in 1863 would have paid him much attention, either. He was a college dropout from the State University in Madison who, in spite of two and one-half years of brilliant scholarship in that institution, was so overcome by a spirit of restlessness that he left his books to spend practically all the rest of his life on the most remote trails not only of the United States and Canada but also of Europe and other parts of the world as well.

Soon after arriving in San Francisco in 1868, he asked a stranger the best way to get out of town. "Where do you wish to go?" the stranger asked.

"Anywhere that's wild," the young man replied.

With a knapsack again on his back he walked eastward through valleys carpeted with flowers and veined with rivers, into the long foothills of the Sierra Nevada mountains, California's loftiest range. Pushing on past lakes and streams, through granite canyons, into the depths of thick forests of fir, pine, and redwoods, he caught sight of the magnificent valley of the Yosemite. Close now to his thirtieth birthday, he was profoundly moved. In his later years he likened the valley to "no temple made with hands" and wrote of it as follows: "From end to end of the temple, from the shrubs and half-buried ferns of the floor to the topmost ranks of jeweled pine spires, it is all one finished unit of divine beauty, weighed in the celestial balances and found perfect."

It was there in the valley of the Yosemite that the thirty-year-old's kinship with nature found its deepest expression. His name was John Muir, who before his death on Christmas Eve, 1914, at the age of seventy-six, was recognized as one of the greatest naturalists of all time. He was a close friend of Ralph Waldo Emerson, President Theodore Roosevelt, and many of the other most famous men of his generation; and it is to him more than almost any other American that we owe the preservation of the Yosemite as a national park. Moreover, it was largely due to President Roosevelt's enthusiasm for Muir's cause (the conservation of the nation's wilderness areas) that before Roosevelt left office in 1909, he increased the nation's total forest preserves from 46,000,000 to more than 148,000,000 acres.

Muir summed up his life in one simple but immortal sentence: "I might have become a millionaire, but I chose to become a tramp." The heritage that this tramp of the Lord made available for his country and for all the world to enjoy is a vast wilderness kingdom that includes some of the noblest manifestations of God's handiwork. We must all do our part in vigorously defending it for the future enjoyment and inspiration of all generations. For there are many who would rob us of it.[2]

[2] This story of John Muir was taken from an article by Brian McGinty, "Friend of the Wilderness: John Muir," *American History Illustrated* (July, 1977), pp. 5-9, 44-48.

Not all the hitchhikers I have met on the highways of America are "tramps of the Lord." But many of them share John Muir's love of nature, and if even one of them could achieve as much as a fraction of what Muir accomplished, it would be a fine contribution to all humanity.

There is something far more important to remember than a love of nature, however. The apostle Paul warned us of this long ago. In his letter to the Romans, he reminded the Christians of Rome that the reason the pagan world had gone so wrong was because instead of worshiping the Creator they had worshiped creation, as personified in their idols—images resembling mortal man, birds, animals, and reptiles. Thus their thinking became futile and their senseless minds were darkened. Therefore, God gave them up to the lusts of their hearts and to all manner of dishonorable passions. What were the results? The results were covetousness, malice, envy, murder, strife, deceit, gossip, slander, hatred of God, insolence, boasting, inventions of evil, disobedience to parents, until the whole culture became foolish, faithless, heartless, ruthless (Romans 1:26-32).

Where could we find a more accurate picture of our own civilization than in the apostle Paul's catalog of the sins of ancient Rome? Concluding his indictment of the pagan people, he said, "Though they know God's decree that those who do such things deserve to die, they not only do them but approve those who practice them" (Romans 1:32). Paul's words sound almost like a summary of the morning and evening news as we hear it reported daily on TV in our own land. It would be best for us if in every American home and in all the secular affairs of the nation we would cry out to God, "What must we do to be saved?" Better still, we should put the question in the first person singular and say in the words of the Philippian jailer as he fell trembling before Paul and Silas in the midst of the earthquake, "What must I do to be saved?" The answer to this question today is the same as it was then. Paul stated it clearly to the terrified jailer at his feet, "Believe in the Lord Jesus, and you will be saved, you and your household" (Acts 16:16-34). If we give heed to this promise and act upon it, we will have gone a long way not only toward the solving of our personal problems but also toward the salvation of our country.

One of the most remarkable testimonies to the need of the human soul for faith in the living God was given to the world by the late Wernher Von Braun, "father of the American space age," shortly before his death in the summer of 1977.

This German-trained physicist, who developed the rockets that carried the first Americans into space and to the moon, said in an extensive Associated Press interview, "Prayer is the most important work of man."[3]

Some months earlier he had stated to a Philadelphia symposium on the essentials of a humane society, "The grandeur of the cosmos serves only to confirm my belief in the certainty of the Creator. . . . It is one thing to accept the natural order as a way of life, but the minute one asks why, then again enters God and all His glory."

Von Braun gave little attention to religion in his native Germany, where he was frequently at odds with the Hitler regime and once went to jail temporarily. It was Von Braun who later developed the ominous V-2 rockets used in the final stages of the war on Britain. Up to that time he had been a nominal Christian. But after he came to the United States, where he became a citizen following the war, his nominal Christianity became an intense commitment. He joined the Episcopal Church, as did his family.

"It was the first time," he said, "I really understood that religion was not just a cathedral inherited from the past or a quick prayer at the last minute. Religion has to be backed up by discipline and effort." Noting that his own prayer life had advanced into a new dimension, he said, "I began to pray daily, hourly, instead of occasionally. I took long rides into the prairie where I could be alone at prayer. I prayed with my wife in the evening."[4]

It is heartening to know that this outstanding scientist, at one time only a nominal Christian, could have had a spiritual experience that made him such a fervent believer in a prayer-hearing God. "Science and religion are not antagonists," he said. "On the contrary, they are sisters. While science tries to learn about the creation, religion tries to better understand the Creator. . . . What strange rationale makes some physicists accept the inconceivable electron as real while refusing to accept the reality of God on the ground that they cannot conceive of Him?"[5]

What rationale indeed? Long ago Jesus said, "I am the way, and the truth, and the life; no one comes to the Father but by me (John 14:16). Philip's puzzled question about that statement was, "Lord, show us the Father, and we shall be satisfied." Jesus said to him, "Have I been with you so long, and yet you do not know me, Philip? He who has seen me has seen the Father" (John 14:8-9).

[3] Associated Press interview, "Science and Religion Are Not Antagonists," *The Arizona Republic* (July, 1977).
[4] *Ibid.*
[5] *Ibid.*

Blessed are we if we have seen the Father as he was revealed to us in Jesus Christ. Like all others among the human race, I have never seen God with the physical eyes. But I have seen him in Christ, and in his church, in my home, in the life and work of godly men and women, and in the grandeur of his creation. Like Wernher Von Braun, I have also gone out into the prairie to be alone with God and "in the rustling grass I hear him pass."[6] For a period of thirty-five years, before my more advanced old age, I used to spend an entire night or sometimes a quiet day in prayer to God beneath the open sky. Sometimes those hours of communion with God were spent on the prairie, as I have said. At other times hours were spent high up at the 14,000-foot level of the Colorado Rockies; on the deck of a ship in midocean; on the cliffs of the North Sea at St. Andrews in Scotland; once alone all night on a golf course; several times at Point Pelee, the southernmost point of Canada on the north shore of Lake Erie, at Leamington, Ontario; another time in the Mojave Desert in Nevada; again in a rowboat on the beautiful lakes of northern Minnesota and Wisconsin; once overlooking the brink of Niagara Falls; now and then in the woods, a hilltop, a meadow, or in my own home; and once in St. Mary's Cathedral, Syracuse, New York. The place is not so important. The main thing is to follow the example of Christ, who often went alone up into the mountains and along the shores of Galilee to be alone with God in prayer through the long and beautiful hours of the night. I commend such a practice to all pilgrims of the night, as for a few years here on earth we are hitchhikers to the Heavenly City whose distant gates we can see from afar.

Thank God for the promise of Jesus as given to us in Matthew 6:6-8, "When you pray, go into your room and shut the door and pray to your Father who is in secret; and your Father who sees in secret will reward you. . . . for your Father knows what you need before you ask him."

And may He help us to know the needs of others and to respond to them. For the tests of the Judgment Day will not be so much the words, doctrines, and professions of our faith. Rather they will be the degree to which we can qualify for the invitation of the Great King when he says in the presence of all nations, "Come, O blessed of my Father, inherit the kingdom prepared for you from the foundation of the world; for I was hungry and you gave me food, I was thirsty and you gave me drink, I was a stranger and you welcomed me, I was naked and you clothed me, I was sick and you visited me, I was in prison and you came to me" (Matthew 25:34-36).

[6] Line from the hymn "This Is My Father's World."

When the righteous were puzzled by this praise and asked him when and where they had done all these things, he replied, "Truly, I say to you, as you did it to one of the least of these my brethren, you did it unto me" (Matthew 25:40).

The owner of a used car may be surprised to hear the Son of man saying to him on Creation's last day, "You may not know me. One day many years ago I was standing by the side of a lonely road. It was near the end of the day, and I was so tired I was ready to drop. Then you came along in your car and gave me a lift. I've got good news for you! There is a kingdom waiting for you, O blessed of my Father."

I can imagine the astonished car owner saying to himself or herself, "What did he mean? I don't remember seeing him by the side of the road."